THE ANCIENT CROSS SHAFTS AT BEWCASTLE AND RUTHWELL

THE ANCIENT CROSS SHAFTS AT BEWCASTLE AND RUTHWELL

ENLARGED FROM

THE REDE LECTURE

delivered before the University of Cambridge on 20 May 1916

BY

THE RIGHT REV. G. F. BROWNE, D.D. (C. & O.), D.C.L., LL.D.

Honorary Fellow, and Formerly Fellow, of St Catharine's College, Vice President of the Society of
Antiquaries of London, formerly Disney Professor of Art and Archaeology in the
University of Cambridge, some time Bishop of Stepney and of Bristol

With Three Photogravures and Twenty-three Illustrations

Cambridge:
at the University Press
1916

CAMBRIDGE
UNIVERSITY PRESS

University Printing House, Cambridge CB2 8BS, United Kingdom

Cambridge University Press is part of the University of Cambridge.

It furthers the University's mission by disseminating knowledge in the pursuit of education, learning and research at the highest international levels of excellence.

www.cambridge.org
Information on this title: www.cambridge.org/9781107536586

© Cambridge University Press 1916

First published 1916
First paperback edition 2015

A catalogue record for this publication is available from the British Library

ISBN 978-1-107-53658-6 Paperback

PREFACE

WHEN the Vice-Chancellor of the University of Cambridge invited me to undertake the responsibility of delivering the Rede Lecture before the University, it was natural that I should hesitate about saying yes. During my twenty-nine years of adult residence at the University, I had heard great men deliver this annual lecture. They began with Airy, Tyndall, Thomson, Ruskin, Max Müller, Huggins, Lockyer, Freeman, and they ended with Huxley, Galton, Lubbock, Seeley, Stokes, and Jebb. Only the common-sense advice of an experienced friend with whom I was staying averted the inevitable no.

In selecting a subject, it seemed right to turn to the branch of study which had been the subject of my lectures for five years in Cambridge when a Professorship had been conferred upon me unsought in 1888. In that branch of study, the Art and Archaeology mainly of our own land, two great monuments stood out very clear in my memory, and I selected them as my subject.

I soon found that since I lectured on these monuments last century the attention of experts had been fixed upon them, and there was an unexpectedly large amount of material to be examined. I had been called away to a Canonry at St Paul's, a Bishopric at Stepney, and a Bishopric at Bristol, and the work of those offices had filled time and thoughts to the almost complete exclusion of the old fascination. Further, I had parted with a very large proportion of my books on leaving a large house at Bristol for a small house at Kensington. But it was too late to draw back. The criticisms and defences of the early date of the two monuments in question had raised all manner of supplementary points, and to deal with all or nearly all of them in an hour was evidently impossible. Accordingly I did what I could to cover the ground, and on May 20, 1916, I read such parts of what I had written as were fairly representative and occupied about 55 minutes. The Essay to which this is the Preface gives the whole.

Three publications must be mentioned, all of them full of information on the subject, all of them opposed to my view. In 1912, Albert S. Cook, Professor of the English Language and Literature in Yale University, published at the Yale University Press, New Haven, Connecticut, an octavo book of 150 pages on *The Date of the Ruthwell and Bewcastle Crosses*. The book is full of interest, and abounds with admirable photographs of the remarkable monuments. It is a book for which an archaeologist may be grateful, and in which those who are not archaeologists may find much interest. That I differ *toto coelo* from the writer only enhances my gratitude for the book. I feel sure that Professor Cook will not misunderstand my non-apologetic manner of treatment of the views which his position and knowledge so fully entitle him to express.

In 1914 Professor Cook added to the debt we owe him a second book of 150 pages, *Some accounts of the Bewcastle Cross between the years 1607 and 1861*, New York, Henry Holt and Company. This useful publication completes our knowledge of the earlier literature on the subject.

In the same year 1914 Dr James King Hewison, of Rothesay, published a very handsome volume, beautifully and copiously illustrated, on *The Runic Roods of Ruthwell and Bewcastle*, with a *Short History of the Cross and Crucifix in Scotland*, Glasgow, John Smith and Son, Ltd. The book is full of illustrative and interesting matter. Like Professor Cook, Dr Hewison assigns a late date to the Crosses. His work has evidently been a labour of love.

Among books that bear helpfully on the general subject I must mention *The Arts in Early England*, Murray, by Professor G. Baldwin Brown the Watson Gordon Professor at Edinburgh, four volumes of which have appeared; and *Byzantine Art and Archaeology*, Oxford, Clarendon Press, by Mr O. M. Dalton of the British Museum.

In the pages of the *Burlington Magazine* there are articles which all who wish to study the subject should read. Sir Martin Conway provides four of these articles, in volumes XXI, XXII, XXIII, XXIV; Professor Lethaby two, XXI and XXIII; Professor Baldwin Brown one, XXIII; Commendatore Rivoira one, XXI; and Messrs Forbes and Dickins one, XXV. There is in these articles a very large preponderance in favour of an early date, not without frank recognition of difficulties.

After I had undertaken the Rede Lecture, Sir Henry Howorth sent me a pamphlet of 19 octavo pages on "The Great Crosses of the 7th Century in Northern England," reprinted from the *Archaeological Journal*. I have postponed the pleasure of reading it until after my Essay is published. It is sure to be full of information and ingenuity, and I preferred to write independently of Sir Henry's work.

I have to thank Mr Tassell of Carlisle for a photograph of the Bewcastle Vine Scrolls, Plate VI, 11, and Mr Gibson of Hexham for a photograph of the principal face of the Ruthwell Cross, Plate V, 9, and much kindness spread over many years. Very special thanks are due to Mr Emery Walker, F.S.A., of 16 Clifford's Inn, Fleet Street, E.C., for his beautiful photogravures of the Ivory Chair of Ravenna and several of the half tone blocks on Plates IV, V, VI, VII. The illustration on page 79 is lent by the Society of Antiquaries. The other illustrations are from my various books dealing directly or indirectly with the subject.

G. F. B.

2 Campden House Road,
Kensington.
July 4, 1916.

CONTENTS

CHAPTER I

PAGE

The Ruthwell and Bewcastle Crosses.—Subjects on the crosses.—Probable date.—Wilfrith and Biscop.—Foreign workmen.—David of Scotland.—Sculpture at Jedburgh.—The Glastonbury obelisks.—The Sandbach Crosses.—Guide-stones.—The Aldhelm Crosses.— Jupiter columns 1

CHAPTER II

Alchfrith of Deira.—The Mercian royal family.—The Bewcastle inscriptions.—The artists of the Bewcastle Cross.—Vietor's date.—Rivoira's view.—Wilfrith's fervour.—His wealth.—The splendours of Ripon.—Resurrection of art in the Kingdoms of the Heptarchy.—Aldhelm of Malmesbury.—Biscop's sacred pictures.—A white marble altar.— A School of Art in Northumbria.—Acca's Cross.—Lombard influence.—Migration of artists.—The tombstone of Trumberecht and "mere guess-work."—The Abercorn and Ethelwold Crosses 15

CHAPTER III

Our Lord in Benediction.—Three branches of early art.—St Cuthbert's coffin.—St John Baptist.—The Ivory Chair of Ravenna.—The Annunciation and the Visitation.—The Flight into Egypt.—The Crucifixion.—The Bird.—Anglo-Saxon coins.—Paul and Antony.—Abbat Hadrian.—The Archer.—The lozenge-shaped O.—St Cuthbert's portable altar.—The dedication stone of St Paul's Jarrow.—The memorial of Ovin.—Acca's Cross.—The Chequers.—The Sundial.—The Falconer.—The Presence of Runes.— Pictish ornament 27

CHAPTER IV

The date of the Ruthwell Cross.—Wide differences between it and the Bewcastle shaft.— The Nimbus.—Didron and Professor Cook.—The Robes of Our Lord.—The Beard.— Wilfrith's journeymen.—Crosses and Altars.—Ancient churchyards.—Triple crosses.— Paulinus.—Antecedent improbability.—Late remains at Durham.—Their bearing on the theories of Cook and Rivoira.—The Caedmon and Bede Crosses . . . 42

CHAPTER V

The ivory chair.—Its history.—Solomon's ivory throne.—Otto III.—Salona and Spalato.— Monograms.—Maximianus.—The subjects of the *tavolette*.—Vine scrolls in Rome.— Eastern *provenance* of the ivory chair.—Biscop and Wilfrith.—The Church of Aurona, Milan.—S. Salvatore, Brescia.—Arian Baptisteries and Crosses.—Controversy on the symbolism of the Lamb.—The Quinisext Council.—Crosses at Bologna and Beverley.— Pre-historic imports from Italy 54

CHAPTER VI

PAGE

The Dream of the Holy Rood.—One of Caedmon's poems.—The Quinisext Council.—
Kedmon mæ fauœđa.—Six readings compared.—The spelling *Kedmon*.—The Cross of
Drahmal.—The word *thun*.—The words *æft, æfter*.—King Oswin.—Phonetic spelling.—
Professor Cook and *Gessus Kristtus*.—*Cynnburug*.—Mistakes in inscriptions.—Local
pronunciation.—Inscriptions not altered like manuscripts.—Lateness of two runes.—
Lul's runic alphabet.—Table of Anglian runes   66

CHAPTER VII

Alchfrith and Aldfrith.—Dr Hewison's arguments.—Stephen Eddi.—Bede.—Fridegoda.—
The Anglo-Saxon Chronicle.—Florence of Worcester.—William of Malmesbury.—Cyniburg and Cuthburg.—Concluding remarks   83

ILLUSTRATIONS

FIG.		PAGE
a.	The Ruthwell Latin Inscriptions	3
b.	The Ruthwell Runes	3
c.	The Bewcastle Runes	4
d.	Monogram of Maximianos	57
e.	The Osgyð stone	79
f.	Table of Anglian runes	82

		PLATE
1.	Maximian's Ivory Chair, front	I
2.	,, ,, ,, back	II
3.	,, ,, ,, sides	III
4.	Figure of Our Lord, Bewcastle	IV
5.	Early Sculpture, Jedburgh	,,
6.	The Bewcastle Shaft	,,
7.	,, ,, ,, ...	V
8.	The Ruthwell Cross	,,
9.	The Washing of the Feet, Ruthwell	,,
10.	Grave Cover, Wirksworth	VI
11.	Vine Scroll, Bewcastle	,,
12.	Tomb-stone, Yarm	,,
13.	Acca's Cross, Hexham	,,
14.	Dedication Stone, Jarrow	VII
15.	The Sandbach Crosses	,,
16.	Cross-head, Durham	,,
17.	The Kirkdale Dial	,,

At the end of the volume

CHAPTER I

The Ruthwell and Bewcastle Crosses.—Subjects on the crosses.—Probable date.—Wilfrith and Biscop.—Foreign workmen.—David of Scotland.—Sculpture at Jedburgh.—The Glastonbury obelisks.—The Sandbach Crosses.—Guide-stones.—The Aldhelm Crosses.—Jupiter columns.

A table of Anglian runes will be found on page 82.

It is nearly 30 years since I first brought before the University the subject of the great crosses at Bewcastle and Ruthwell. The occasion was the inaugural lecture in the Senate House on my appointment as Disney Professor of Archaeology, in the early part of 1888. During the five years tenure of that office, I dealt steadily with the sculptured stones of England, Scotland, Ireland, Wales, and Man, from various points of view, history, art, language, script, besides many investigations of parallel examples in various parts of Europe. There is not, in my knowledge, in any other country, anything to compare with the continuous series of Sculptured and Inscribed Stones in these islands from the earliest times of our Christianity. The English stones form a great consistent whole, endless in variety, varying greatly, too, in interest, but moving steadily on from age to age. There has been serious decadence, especially in regard to the presentation of the human form; art has never since risen to so high a point in this respect as was attained by the artists of Bewcastle and Ruthwell. On the other hand there was remarkable advance in the development of interlacements and other decorative methods of occupying surfaces on memorial and monumental stones. But there has been sufficient continuity to make it impossible to take a group of 7th century stones, especially inscribed stones, and dump them down in the 12th century, as some modern writers have proposed to do. Since the year 1892 I have published in two or three books a good deal of matter in this connection, chiefly in my *Conversion of the Heptarchy* for the Bewcastle Cross and in *Theodore and Wilfrith* for the Ruthwell Cross, and in *St Aldhelm* for sculptures in the south-west.

My aim in the Disney Lectures was to make the subjects interesting, with enough on the scientific side to justify their treatment in professorial lectures in the University and to suggest scientific study of many of the problems which the subjects afforded. The twenty-four years which have passed since those lectures ceased have seen much attention given to some of the problems then dealt with. For the last four or five years these two crosses have been a prominent feature in the discussion of our earliest mediaeval art by learned experts.

It has been a pleasure to me to see from time to time that all monuments or inscriptions in these islands, which I have seen mentioned in the various discussions, were dealt with in the course of my lectures; as were, also, the principal illustrations from continental art. And I do not remember to have seen reason to correct anything of importance which was said on any of the almost endless points then raised and discussed. I did some years ago, in consequence of a criticism, alter in my stereotype plates my remarks on one Anglo-Saxon word. I have now to withdraw that alteration and abide by the original utterance.

During my tenure of the Disney Professorship, my University work in other spheres was so manifold and so continuous and exacting that I had not opportunity for really scientific study on an elaborate scale. It is needless to say that the twenty-one years of a bishop's life which have followed have not supplied the opportunity which the life in Cambridge lacked. It needs an apology for one long ago *donatus rude* to enter the arena again, occupied as it now is with gladiators thoroughly trained and equipped.

The
Ruthwell
Cross

The subjects on the face and the back of the Ruthwell Cross* are these: a bird, an archer, the Baptist with the Lamb, the Lord treading on the heads of beasts, Paul the first hermit breaking bread with Antony in the desert, the Flight into Egypt, a man with a bird, the Visitation, the woman washing the Lord's feet, the healing of the man blind from his birth, the Annunciation, the Crucifixion.

The rims of the panels on the shaft containing these subjects have inscriptions in beautiful capitals, describing in Latin the subjects represented. The accompanying figure, *a*, shews the inscriptions describing the washing of the feet and the healing of the blind man. The illustration is taken by photography from my rubbing.

The inscription is taken from the Vulgate Version of St Luke vii. 37, 38, *attulit alabastrum unguenti et stans retro secus pedes eius lacrimis coepit rigare pedes eius et capillis capitis sui tergebat*, in our Authorised Version "brought an alabaster box of ointment, and stood at his feet behind him weeping, and began to wash his feet with tears, and did wipe them with the hairs of her head." The statement that the woman anointed the feet with the unguent follows this in each case. Thus the scene is not correctly described as the "Anointing of the Feet," the actual representation shews the "Washing of the Feet."

* Plate V. 8, 9.

Professor Cook (see *Preface*) misreads the inscription. He prints the last letter of *tergebat* as A, with a horizontal line above it to indicate the omission of the T. But the T is there, fitted into the lower half of the A. This mistake misses the interesting connection with the manuscripts of our earliest period, where letters are tucked away in small

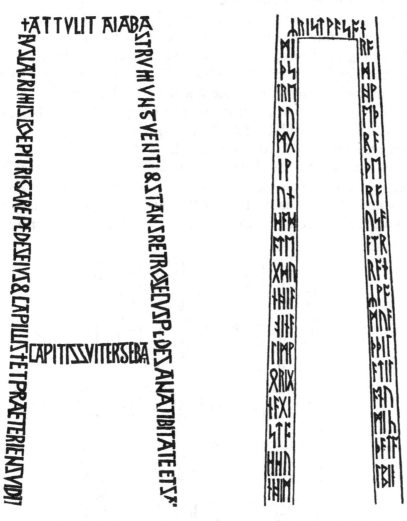

a. Ruthwell, Latin   *b.* Ruthwell, Runes

size into void places, in a curious and puzzling way. It misses also the connection with another feature of our earliest ornamentation of manuscripts to which I call attention in my remarks on the *g* rune at Bewcastle. The ordinary A leaves of necessity a void space in the upper part of the line, and in our early ornamental script a bold horizontal line is placed across the top of the A, as will be seen in the figure under consideration.

Thus from a palaeographical point of view the misreading of the inscription in this one letter is a serious flaw.

The inscription round the panel below, *et praeteriens vidit . . . . a natibitate et sa . . . .* relates to the scene in the panel, the healing of the blind man. Only the early part of the inscription is a direct quotation from the Gospel story in the 9th chapter of St John.

The two edges of the shaft are occupied by continuous vine scrolls, with birds and animals full of life enjoying the fruit. The rims are occupied by Anglian runes, giving portions of the great Anglo-Saxon poem known as the *Dream of the Holy Rood*. The second figure, *b*, shews the runes containing the portion of the poem which begins with "Christ was on the Cross." The whole poem is given in Chapter VI. A table of runes and their equivalents will be found on page 82.

The
Bewcastle
shaft

The Bewcastle shaft* has the Baptist, the Lord in Benediction, a man with a bird, panels with interlacements, foliage scrolls, grape scrolls, a sundial, a long panel of chequers, and one whole side occupied by a vine scroll with birds and animals as at Ruthwell. There is one long inscription in runes, above the man with the bird and presumably referring to him;

c. Bewcastle Runes

* Plates IV. 6, V. 7.

above the Lord's head is Gessus Kristtus in runes, and on the horizontal bands separating the panels there are short runic inscriptions. The accompanying figure, *c*, shews a reading of six lines of the inscription, produced in the same manner as *a* and *b*. I return to this inscription later on, at page 16.

These two monuments have on them three-fifths of all the Anglian runic inscriptions. The remaining two-fifths are on 19 monuments, some being mere scraps. Three are in one churchyard.

The Ruthwell Cross is 17 ft. 6 in. high. The Bewcastle shaft is 14 ft. 6 in. high, and its cross-head was 2 ft. 6 in., 17 ft. in all.

The occurrence, on the Bewcastle Cross, of the names of several persons Probable well known in the second half of the 7th century, and the mention of date the first year of a king, appeared to indicate the year 670 as the date of that cross. The striking similarity of the representations of our Lord and the Baptist on the shaft at Ruthwell to those at Bewcastle suggested contemporary workmanship, while striking differences between these two great runic monuments suggested some moderate difference of date, and pointed to a period of rapid development, artistic and religious.

If we are right in the main in our readings of the runes on the Bewcastle Cross, that ancient monument appears to account for the mysterious disappearance of Alchfrith the sub-king of Deira, one of the puzzles of our early history. Apart from any inscription, it seems clear that some personage of high position and importance is represented in the sculpture. I have not seen any suggestion of any probable person other than Alchfrith.

It is not too much to say that everything we know in any detail of the history of Northumbria and the Northumbrians, their church work and their script, nearly before and nearly after the year 670, fits in curiously completely with the phenomena of these monuments.

Two remarkable men stood out in the early years of the Northumbrian Wilfrith Church, Wilfrith the bishop and Biscop the abbat. Both were born in the short reign of Oswald, King and Saint. Together they set out to visit Rome, as very young men, in 652 or 653. They went by way of Lyon, the most venerable ecclesiastical centre in France. Thence they went to Rome. Wilfrith had been trained at Lindisfarne in the Scotic usages, but with all the zest of a convert he threw himself into the usages which— as he said at the Conference of Whitby—they found practised in Italy and Gaul, and knew to be the rule in Africa, Asia, Egypt, Greece, the whole Christian world. Inasmuch as I am relying mainly upon eastern evidences in support of the early date of the Ruthwell Cross, I wish at the outset to emphasise that pointed reference to the church outside the church of the West. We shall come upon references to the profound impression, religious and artistic, which this visit to Rome produced upon an enthusiastic young man, whose father and mother had been pagan Angles. For the rest, I will only note here that on his return journey Wilfrith spent three years at Lyon. Some years ago I examined Le Blant's inscriptions in Gaul, to see if at or near Lyon there were examples of early Christian lapidary art which might have influenced him in the direction of the art of Bewcastle and Ruthwell. I found that there were in his time at Ansa, and at Briod, and in Lyon itself, notably in the subterranean chapel under St Irénée, examples of scrolls with leaves and birds. But of course the full impulse came from what he saw in Italy. Indeed it would need very special pleading to attribute any influence in the direction of the vine scrolls of Bewcastle to these dull and formal and poor examples from the Lyonnaise.

Biscop

The other great originator of noble church work and art was Benedict Biscop, a Northumbrian noble, born about 638 in Oswald's reign. He was a minister or attendant of King Oswy, and had received from him a grant of land for his maintenance. This he resigned at the age of 25, that he might visit the tombs of the Apostles St Peter and St Paul, those tombs of the twin Apostles being the great attraction to Rome, the Apostolic See because of the tombs of these Apostles. He visited Rome six times, in five journeys from England. He brought back great quantities of MSS., relics, pictures, everything that was needed for the full equipment of the church. He had agents buying for him in Europe. He founded and equipped the twin monasteries of Wearmouth and Jarrow. Among other treasures, he brought robes of silk and illuminated manuscripts so rich that the king bought them from him by great grants of land.

Foreign
workmen

It is a notable fact that these great ecclesiastics employed workmen from Italy and Gaul. Considering the extreme stiffness of such decorative remains as we have in Gaul proper, I have always been inclined to think that Cisalpine Gaul may have been the district from which the Gaulish workmen came; and the beautiful freedom of the work they did here suggests that by chance or of set purpose artists with Byzantine training were chosen.

Rival date

I have often asked those who dispute the early date of these monuments to name some other period the conditions of which fit in with these phenomena. The answer has been given by an American, Professor Cook of Yale, and he has recently been supported by an Italian, Commendatore Rivoira. These two archaeologists, men, I need not say, of very great knowledge, name the 12th century, Professor Cook attributing the erection of the two monuments to one and the same man, David, Prince of Cumbria 1107, King David I of Scotland 1124–1153. Professor Cook holds that one after another of the subjects on the Ruthwell Cross cannot be found in Christian Art at anything like so early a date as the seventh century. This has been completely disproved.

In contrast with the period of Wilfrith, it is not too much to say that scarcely anything—if anything—which we know in detail of the history, the church work, the language, and the script, of David and his surroundings, fits in with the phenomena of these monuments. Indeed the whole tone and air of the great shafts cry out against any such attribution.

David was the son of Malcolm Canmore, whose father Duncan was overthrown by Macbeth. His mother was the English Margaret, sister of Edgar the Atheling. He became an English nobleman by his marriage with Matilda daughter of Waltheof, Earl of Northumberland, by Judith, niece of William the Conqueror. He lived as a young man at the court of his brother-in-law, the distinguished Norman scholar, Henry I of England, surnamed Beauclerc. As the leading English noble he was the first of the nobles to swear allegiance to his niece, Henry's daughter, the Empress Maud, and later on he knighted his great-nephew, afterwards Henry II of England. He was thoroughly Norman in his views of church and of state. He introduced the Norman feudal system into Cumbria, as its Prince. As King, he continued his mother's church policy in Scotland, completing the removal of the ancient Culdee system by building great abbeys and founding five of the Scottish sees. In all the remains of the churches which he built, I am not aware that any sculpture has been found that has any artistic or other connection with the shafts at Bewcastle and Ruthwell. Being so great a church builder as he was, we may take it as certain that if he gave to the world those beautiful pieces of lapidary sculpture, some of their characteristics would have been stamped upon his creations elsewhere.

The most beautiful piece of work of this character which we possess, coming from any part connected with David's great church work, was found at Jedburgh*. It is quite beautiful enough, and quite simple enough, to have been carved by the skilled mason who carved the vine scrolls at Bewcastle and Ruthwell, with happy creatures enjoying the fruit. But instead of its being an argument in favour of David as the author of those great monuments, it is a conclusive argument against him. Only this year, Mr C. H. Peers, on the part of the Board of Works, has been repairing

David of Scotland

Sculpture at Jedburgh

* Plate IV. 5.

the tower of the ancient church at Jedburgh, contemporary with—at least not later than—David. He found embedded in the original rubble core of the tower a piece of the same work. Thus David's workmen were destroying not erecting these beautiful things at important centres of church work. I need not dwell upon the fact that in David's time long inscriptions in ancient Anglian runes were completely, hopelessly, out of date.

This design from Jedburgh was adopted by Sir William Richmond for the six clerestory windows on the north and south in the Choir of St Paul's, an angel taking the place of each of the happy little creatures. At Spalato we have in the scrolls at the side of one of the great doors a man standing upright in each alternate scroll, holding on by a portion of the stem of the scroll. I have not myself found any other example of this. At Lincoln and in other places we have armed sportsmen among the scrolls, but that is a different idea.

Obelisks at Glastonbury   We have the direct evidence of a contemporary of David of Scotland that there were in his time in the south of England monuments of this character but on a larger scale, described then as very ancient. William of Malmesbury, who wrote from 1100 to about 1140 and died in 1143, tells us of the Antiquity of Glastonbury. I dealt with this in one of my Disney lectures, delivered Feb. 7, 1888.

One of the abbats, Tica, had fled from Northumbria before the Danes, in 754, and had brought with him relics of many Northumbrian saints, of Bishop Aidan, of Hilda, of five abbats of Wearmouth, and so on *. Tica was eventually buried in a tomb which William describes as *arte celaturae non ignobilis*, with an epitaph which he had read, setting forth that the tomb was 'constructed with marvellous beauty,' as though, one may suggest, he had brought with him patterns from Lindisfarne and Wearmouth. That, however, though it accounts for one or two of the names to be mentioned, is not the point that concerns our present enquiry. William proceeds to tell us that Arthur and his wife were buried there, between two 'pyramids,' obelisks, or pillars, identifying it with Avalon, the place of dim mysterious romance, and that king Kenwin† was buried with one 'pyramid,' *nobiliter exsculpta*. These three pyramids appear to be distinct from the two lofty shafts next mentioned ‡. He proceeds:

* Two accounts are given of the date of the conveyance of relics from the north, the other placing it about 940. It is one of the numerous apparent inconsistencies of William's texts, due no doubt to revisers who had a purpose of their own to serve. In this case the inconsistency does not affect the truth of the other details relating to Tica.

† Kentwine of Wessex died in 685. He married a sister of Eormenburh, the wife of Ecgfrith of Northumbria, Alchfrith's brother. This connection is worthy of note.

‡ See further on pages 9 and 10.

"I would gladly know what almost no one knows anything about, what the meaning is of those two pyramids which stand a few feet from the ancient church *. One is 26 feet high, and has five tiers, or storeys, *tabulatus* †. It is very ancient, but it has on it things which can be clearly read though not clearly understood. On the top panel is an *imago* in pontifical dress; on the next an *imago* with the pomp of a king, and certain letters ‡. In the third § and fourth ‖ there are names. In the fifth and lowest, an *imago* and an inscription ¶. The other pyramid is 18 feet high and has four storeys, with these inscriptions, Heddi Episcopus Bregored Beorward. I would not rashly say what these signify, but I suspect the bones are contained within, in hollowed stones, of the persons whose names are inscribed on the outside." Thus far William. Logperesbeorh was the Saxon name of Montacute in Somerset. Bregored was the next abbat of Glastonbury but one to the abbat of the year 601. Beorhtwald was abbat in Theodore's time and became Archbishop of Canterbury after him in 693. Hedde was bishop of the West Saxons 676–705. Wilfrith's life covered all these dates. He died in 709. Leland visited these obelisks. He became the king's antiquary in 1533 and died in 1552. The pillars were greatly perished in his time, so that even with a magnifying glass he could barely make out enough to follow the description of William of Malmesbury. Willis ** says that the two crosses were standing in 1771. I have traced a portion of one of them down to 1790, but I fear it is now wholly lost. When last mentioned it was a gate post at the entrance to the Abbey enclosure.

There is a good deal to be said on the passage above quoted which contains the statement that king Arthur and his queen Guinevere were buried between the two pyramids first mentioned. In William's first edition—so to call it—of the *Gesta Regum*, in 1125, he says definitely that the place of Arthur's sepulture is unknown, and he retained that statement in later revisions. Further, in quoting from the *De Antiquitate* in another work the parts relating to Avalon, he omits this passage and yet refers his reader to this treatise. Further still, he condemns elsewhere the practice of giving heed to British traditions, and here he gives the substance of the Arthurian legends. The inference is irresistible that this Arthurian

Arthurian legends

---

* Ini of Wessex, the brother of Aldfrith's wife Cuthburg, had built a new church at Glastonbury.
† The *tavolette* of Maximian's chair at Ravenna.
‡ Her Sexi Blisyer.
§ Wemerest Bantomp Pinepegn; Gale prints the last name thus; in the MS. the first *p* is a *w*, and the second a *th*, Wine Thegn.
‖ Hats Pulfred Eanfled; the *p* is again *w* in the MS.; these two names are very Northumbrian.
¶ Logpor Peslicas et Bregden Spelpes Hyin Gendes Bern.
** *Architectural History of Glastonbury*, Cambridge, page 30.

and Avalonian legend is an interpolation of later time. This again does not in the least affect anything that William tells us in the second passage quoted above*. Mr Newell, to whose paper I refer in a note, in each case interprets "pyramids" as "crosses." I much prefer the word—and idea —obelisks. Surely William knew a cross when he saw it.

We may fairly argue that Abbat Tica brought with him from Northumbria the latest developments of the dragonesque school of surface ornamentation. The fact that the West-Saxon standard was a dragon, witness Harold's standard at Senlac on the Bayeux "Tapestry," and that the symbol of the chief foes of the West Saxons, the Britons on their western border, had also the dragon as their symbol, would naturally lead to the adoption of this branch of Northumbrian art. We have very striking examples of this style of decoration in Somerset and in adjoining districts. The sculptures at Ramsbury, Rowberrow, West Camel, Dolton, Gloucester, and Colerne, will be found in my *St Aldhelm*. Some of them are very striking. All bear upon our main subject.

Glastonbury is a delightful place, but no one will credit it with being a district likely to preserve ancient stone pillars by the dryness of its atmosphere. A pillar of north country grit, in dry north country air, might well expect to live in good form more than half as long again.

It is an interesting fact, which Professor Cook might have used with some force in his attribution of the Bewcastle and Ruthwell shafts to David of Scotland, that David's great-nephew, for whom he fought and whom he knighted, is said to have opened the tomb of Arthur in the cemetery of Glastonbury when he became king as Henry II. One chronicle tells us that in the excavation of the supposed tomb by Abbat Henry, about 1191, a leaden cross was found bearing the legend *Hic iacet inclitus rex Arturus in insula Avallonia sepultus*. Giraldus Cambrensis adds the words *cum Winnevereia uxore sua secunda*, and states that the investigation was undertaken by the advice of Henry II, who had been told by an old British bard that Arthur was buried between the two obelisks. It has been assumed to be fatal to this story that Henry II died 1189, two years before the investigation; but that is not inconsistent with his having advised it before his death. It seems probable that the story was a monkish invention—to the extent of depicting the piece of lead—and that the interpolation in William's account of Glastonbury was part of the proceedings.

I have dwelt upon these points, partly because of the interest naturally attaching to Arthurian legends, but mainly in order to meet the

---

* See a useful paper by William Wells Newell, in the *Proceedings of the Modern Language Association of America*, 1903, Vol. XVIII, pages 459–512.

possible objection to my claim of priority for the Glastonbury obelisks over Bewcastle and Ruthwell, that in quoting William's account of what he actually saw I am quoting from a source tainted by inconsistencies. The whole story of the very ancient *imagines* and inscriptions—very ancient as compared with the memorials of king Kentwine and other 7th century persons—stands untouched.

I have not seen mention of these remarkable fore-runners and con- The temporaries of the Bewcastle Cross by any of the writers who have dealt Sandbach Crosses with the question; and yet they have a decided bearing upon it. Nor, again, have I seen mention made of two noble shafts, still standing after vicissitudes worse than those which have so sorely damaged the Ruthwell Cross. I refer to the great columns standing in the market place at Sandbach in Cheshire, a view of which is given on Plate VII.

The larger cross is now 16 ft. 8 in. high, including 10 inches of the circular head which has been about 3 ft. in diameter, making the cross when complete above 19 ft. high. The breadth at the base is 2 ft. 7 in., one edge being 2 ft. and the other 1 ft. 10 in. The smaller cross has 10 ft. 9 in. of its shaft remaining, having lost length both at top and bottom. There is a piece of the head cemented on at the top, about 1 ft. 2 in. The breadth at the broken off base is 2 ft. 1½ in. by 1 ft. 8½ in. The height of the smaller cross must have been about 16 ft. I delivered a Disney lecture on these crosses on Feb. 14, 1888*. On this present occasion I must only mention some of the subjects.

On the larger cross there is a great crucifixion, with the heads of the evangelists' symbols in the four angles, the figure clothed to below the hips. There is the manger scene. There is a man head downwards, denoting overthrow. There are two sets of three figures, the central figure dominant. On the opposite face is the Annunciation, Mary seated, with a distaff. There is Our Lord led bound, and Simon carrying the Cross. There are two panels of dragons, their tongues and members much intertwined. On one of the sides there are 11 figures standing on supports projecting right and left from a central stem. Bearing down upon them from above is a very fine dragon with tongue triply cloven, evidently the descent of the Holy Ghost upon the eleven original apostles. On the opposite side is a great waving stem with tendrils, like the trees of life at Ruthwell and Bewcastle, but the tendrils end in all sorts of horrid creatures apparently in great delight, and there is a rude figure of a man

* My lecture was printed by the Cambrian Archaeological Association in *Archæologia Cambrensis* in April 1910, pages 283–304, with 15 illustrations from my outlined rubbings and 7 photographs of details of the crosses.

with his feet about half way up the tree. I suggested 28 years ago that this is the twelfth apostle, Judas, about to hang himself on the tree of death. I abide by that suggestion. The smaller cross is similar in character, but it has long strings of very good interlacements running up the rims of the broad sides. It has the descent of the Spirit upon twelve apostles similarly staged; the Spirit is in the form of two interlaced dragons.

The larger of these crosses must be taken, I think, to be a teaching cross, erected early in the Christian history of Mercia. I can have no doubt that it was a well known and ancient monument in the time of David of Scotland. The smaller cross is less meaning and differs a good deal in its arrangements, but the figures of men are very much the same as on the larger cross. The two are on an old platform, with short carved posts at the corners. As the platform is some 4 ft. high, the total height is sufficient to make it not an agreeable task to hang on the top in a storm of driving sleet, examining with eye and finger the sadly perished details, as I had to do, tied on with rope.

In Cheshire, towards the Derbyshire borders, there was for some reason or other a practice of setting up two stone pillars side by side, usually cylindrical, with the upper part cut into four faces like a lead pencil, the faces being sculptured. They were so near each other that they were let into the same stone as a socket, one pillar being taller than the other. They were apparently used to mark the way across the moors. One can understand two crosses being placed at the head and foot of a grave, the one taller and more massive than the other, but the reason of these pairs of cylindrical stones I have never been able to discover, or guess with any feeling of confidence. The two great Sandbach Crosses seem to have been erected on the same principle, whatever that principle may have been. My solution is, that these little pillars served not only as guide-posts, but as compasses, the taller being always, say, at the northern end of the little platform*. There are, I am told, examples of obelisks thus arranged; and we may remember the description of the circus races in the letter of Cassiodorus—to call him still by that name—when Theodoric bestowed a monthly allowance on Thomas the Charioteer: "The obelisks raise their height towards the sky; the loftier is dedicated to the sun, the lower to the moon."

There are no stones in England, Ireland, or Scotland, or so far as

* I am told that gypsies indicate to their friends who are following the way they have gone by setting up two sticks a few feet apart. The line in which they are set shews the line of route, and the taller stick shews the way they have gone. At cross-roads two sticks are laid in the form of a cross, one with one limb longer than the other; the longer limb shews which road has been taken.

I know anywhere, with which we can compare either of the Sandbach crosses in the way of resemblances. As to the place where they are found, it is within a few miles of the accepted site of the battle of Feathanleag, where, in the year 584, Ceaulin was defeated in the great fight with the British, which not only broke the West Saxon power, but rolled back the whole tide of conquest for a time. Ceaulin's brother Cutha was killed in this battle. It is very near the point at which the ancient way from the north-east, from Isurium to Deva, turned due west on coming near Chester, and I suppose it is by no means unlikely that on the occasion of Ethelfrith's invasion, which ended in the battle of Chester in 613, there was a serious fight in the marshy ground to the north-east of this place. The local belief is that they commemorate the introduction of Christianity into Mercia in 653, when the king's son brought back his Christian bride and four priests, two of whom were Cedda and Ceadda (Chad). There is a very curious account of these crosses in King's *Vale Royal* published at Chester in 1656. The account, quoting an earlier account, states that there are certain images and writings engraved thereon, which, as they say, a man cannot read except he be holden with his head downwards; and this verse, as they hold opinion, is engraved thereon,

> In Sandbach, by the sandy ford,
> Lieth the ninth part of Dublin's hord*,
> Nine to or nine fro
> Take me down or else I fall.

"Certain I am that on Sunday mᵍ, Nov. 1, 1561, there were 3 chests of tinne or such like metal found near the said river, but nothing in them. On the covers were certain letters or characters engraved."

This reference in local tradition of the sixteenth and seventeenth century to a quantity of money brought from Dublin and lost at Sandbach, where the road crosses a slack marshy place at a point of the stream well described by the name "the sandy ford," a likely place for an accident to heavy treasure chests or for a military disaster, is very curious, at a time when we might have supposed that all trace had been lost among the country people of the fact that the same man was King of Danish Dublin and King of Danish Northumbria, and passed and repassed this way each time he went from one of his capitals to the other.

The Sandbach Crosses are of the utmost importance as illustrating the principle and practice of great crosses setting forth the facts of the New Testament. They seem to me to be independent of all known types, the work of native genius. They may not in themselves illustrate our

---

* Hord means treasure; horde for a mass of men had not then been introduced.

period 670 to 700 or thereabouts; though it is impossible to regard them as other than very ancient relics of Anglian times. But I have a very apt illustration from that very period, the details of which I worked out in my book on the life and times of St Aldhelm, thirteen years ago.

St Aldhelm, my predecessor at Malmesbury, and according to William of Malmesbury one of the three most learned men of the Anglo-Saxons, was thirty years old when Alchfrith the sub-king of Northumbria disappeared. At that date he was attending the lectures of Theodore and Hadrian at Canterbury. He became the first bishop of Sherborne in 705, and he died in the same year as Wilfrith, 709. He died at a distance, by road, of fifty miles from Malmesbury. They carried him home by stages, taking seven days to do it. At each place where the body rested for the night, they afterwards set up a stone cross. All of these crosses were in existence, and unbroken, when William of Malmesbury wrote of them four hundred years after they were set up. Some sixteen years ago I calculated as closely as I could the probable resting-places, seven miles apart, on the way from Doulting in Somerset where he died to the cloister at Malmesbury where his remains lay till the dissolution. At five of the places I found remains of Anglo-Saxon sculptured stones, very beautiful sculptures in one case, in another case two pieces of a massive shaft, with unusual patterns and one or two letters in large Latin capitals of excellent design*. We could not well have more direct evidence of the wide-spread practice of erecting sculptured and inscribed memorial shafts and crosses in the generation which produced the Bewcastle and Ruthwell shafts.

Before leaving contemporary and earlier examples of memorial columns, inscribed and decorated, of like character with that at Bewcastle, it would be natural to glance further back still and note such monuments as the Cat (battle) Stane near Edinburgh, with its Vetta and Victis, and the monument at Horsted which bore the name of their better known relative Horsa. But that would lead to much digression not bearing upon decorative work. Less far apart from our subject would be some reference to columns adorned with vine tendrils and vine scrolls, with birds and little creatures, of a date long anterior to 670. These are the "Jupiter columns" of Germany, dated by the experts from the close of the second to the middle of the third century A.D., presumably Roman adaptations of Germanic symbolism, as of a column or a tree supporting the sky or reaching to the gods†.

* The capital A on this shaft is 3 inches long, the same length as the great A in Acca's name on the Acca Cross at Hexham.

† I owe much interesting information on these Juppitergigantensäulen to Mr A. B. Cook, Fellow of Queens' College.

CHAPTER II

Alchfrith of Deira.—The Mercian royal family.—The Bewcastle inscriptions.—The artists of the Bewcastle Cross.—Vietor's date.—Rivoira's view.—Wilfrith's fervour.—His wealth.—The splendours of Ripon.—Resurrection of art in the Kingdoms of the Heptarchy.—Aldhelm of Malmesbury.—Biscop's sacred pictures.—A white marble altar.—A School of Art in Northumbria.—Acca's Cross.—Lombard influence.—Migration of artists.—The tombstone of Trumberecht and "mere guess-work."—The Abercorn and Ethelwold Crosses.

The combination on one monument of the names Alchfrith, Kynnburug, Kyneswitha, and Wulfhere Mercian King, with a mention on the same monument of the first year of a king of the land in which the monument is placed, with the name Ecgfrith, is far too solid a fact for any special pleading as to whether there should be an *n* or an *i* in the middle of Kynnburug, and whether *u* is or is not a termination possible in the 7th century. The Anglo-Saxon speech in that district was no doubt then as the English of that district now is, and as the Emperor Sigismund claimed to be, *super grammaticam.* Twentieth century precision is one thing, seventh century roughness is another thing. The ordinary mortal is inclined to think that roughness is an argument for an early date and decidedly against such date and conditions as those of David, prince or king. Until another interpretation is provided, consistent with the conditions of the date to which it is asserted to belong, the king in memory of whom the cross was erected was Alchfrith son of Oswy; his queen was Kyniburga, her sister was Kyneswitha, their brother was Wulfhere the Mercian king. Of the fact that the date indicated by our reading of the runes was 670, there is of course no question, if our reading is correct.

We are told by the critics that only very few words can be read on the Bewcastle Cross in addition to the very legible words Gessus Kristtus, namely *Alcfrithu, Ecgfrithu, Kynnburug*; and Oswy's name is allowed to be probably there. But *fruman gear* was quite clear thirty years ago, with Kyninges above it and Ecgfrithu above that, the very words that give the date 670. And whatever may now be the case with the main inscription when viewed on the spot, I can only say that a large number of the runes are very easily read in the photographs given by Professor Cook. Lord Salisbury once allayed anxieties as to delimitations in foreign parts by telling his anxious critics to look at "a large map," with its expansion of territory.

In the supposed illegible inscription at Bewcastle, I recommend a small photograph, with its concentration of lettering. Even Cook's larger photograph, fig. 21, is in its upper lines legible; the smaller photograph, fig. 20, one-third linear, is clearer still. Wherever the runes can be read on the photograph, they agree with the reading which I for the present accept as in the main worthy of respect. I may add that when I visited the stone I took a rubbing of the six lower lines of the large inscription, the other lines being beyond the reach of my arm, and except in the decayed parts of the lowest line the blank spaces in the rubbing, shewing the actual shape of each rune, supported the reading, while the decayed parts did not contradict it. Fig. *c*, page 4, gives my outlined rubbing, reproduced by photography. The rubbing of *fruman gear* also seemed to be quite clear. It is not possible to mistake such runes as *s, t, e, g, u*, if there are any grooves at all left in the decay of a runic inscription. There are grooves enough left at Bewcastle to satisfy any investigator.

Stephens's suggestion of the reading of the Bewcastle runes, other than the GESSUS KRISTTUS, was as follows:—

†This sigbecn thun setton hwætred wothgar olwfwolthu aft alchfrithu ean küning eac oswiung + gebid heo sinna sowhula.

†This slender token of victory Hwætred Wothgar Olwfwolthu set up in memory of Alchfrith a king and son of Oswy † Pray for the high sin of his soul.

Beyond question, the runes are very indistinct in the lowest lines, but it seems to me clear that there is a bidding of prayer for the soul, as at Thornhill and elsewhere. My illustration begins with the *gar* of *Wothgar*.

On the horizontal bands on the other faces Stephens reads

Fruman gear küninges rices thæs Ecgfrithu.
Künnburug Küneswitha Mürcna Küng Wulfere.

Illegible
runes

It is said that the runes of our reading are only to be read at all because they have been painted in on the stone. As far as records go, what happened was this. Some one, some long time ago, washed the whole inscription over with some composition intended to arrest the decay which was then serious. In course of time this composition disappeared under stress of weather, excepting in the grooves of the runes, where it had settled and was preserved. When I examined the stone, the dark colour shewed clearly in the grooves, which were still very deep, but I did not see traces of it elsewhere. My rubbing naturally took no count of the colour deep down in the grooves, and I need not say that if there had been any paint where there was no groove my rubbing would not shew a blank space at that point.

In furtherance of the argument that the grooves of the so-called illegible runes at Bewcastle are to be trusted, it should be remarked that the runes on the cross-head now lost were so clear in 1617, that people who did not know runes copied them as they would copy a diagram and we can read their copy now quite easily, in exactly the runes as we now read them on the shaft of the cross.

As we shall see in Chapter VI, the learned runist Wilhelm Vietor *Vietor's date* disputes many or most of our readings of the Bewcastle Cross, and, so far as that goes, rejects the historical connections which we assert. But at the same time he states his conviction, based on the whole air of the monument, that it cannot be put later than 750. On the whole it may fairly be said that if the runes are taken to be so illegible that not a word of all the historical connection can be substantiated, the most experienced experts will continue to allow to the Bewcastle shaft at least the probability of its late 7th century date.

The shaft at Bewcastle has in some of its panels problems which are *Puzzling problems* gravely puzzling, if we are to link it in period with Ruthwell. It seems to me that apart from Wilfrith's artists, and indeed before they set to work on a large scale here, there must have been artists who combined with the stately images and the vine scrolls of Italy and the East patterns much out of harmony with Wilfrith's altered views, more in harmony with Scotic Lindisfarne. And that raises a question which has been, so far as I know, overlooked. Whence came the desire of the two Northumbrian youths, the Lindisfarne scholar and the Court noble, to go to Rome? The idea suggests itself to me, as I try to read between the lines, that visitors from Italy had wandered to these islands, possibly artists who because their business had been broken up by local wars, had found their way to Northumbria. What they had to tell to the very keen young churchmen there would inspire the passionate desire to go and see. Meanwhile the visitors remained here and created a school of art workers. The dates would give them twenty years before they and their pupils set to work upon Bewcastle, where the foreign and the local are combined so curiously as to demand some such explanation. The local element was eliminated before the Ruthwell triumph was achieved. That seems to me to save the phenomena, in the old astronomical phrase.

Commendatore Rivoira has a remark in his most interesting article *Rivoira's view* on these crosses in the *Burlington Magazine*, XXI. 15, which calls for notice. He says, "Now we may be certain, for there is documentary evidence of the fact, that until Biscop brought his craftsmen from France for S. Peter's, Monkwearmouth (675), and Wilfrid between 672 and 678 erected and

Northumbrian fervour

decorated S. Andrew's, Hexham, with craftsmen drawn specially from Italy, and from France as well, the arts of building and carving had sunk to a very low level in the British isles; otherwise Biscop and Wilfrid—especially the latter—would never have gone to the serious expense of bringing builders and artists from a distance." Those last words explain Rivoira's inability to understand the conditions. He has no idea of the marvellous vitality and determination of the Northumbrians, the latest of the new comers. Nor can he conceive the passionate fervour of Wilfrith in his love for the best church art. If the best could not be produced at home, he must bring it from abroad, for the best he would have. To talk of the serious expense is an injustice to the memory of this great man. And Rivoira takes no count of the fact that to Wilfrith and his contemporaries Christianity was a new and precious treasure, above gold and precious stones, above life itself. To set it forth in its highest perfection of beautiful art was not merely a duty, it was a delight, an obsession if you will, a passion. Nor does he seem to realise the marvellous—all-explaining—expansion of mind and sense and soul, that a dominant nature like Wilfrith's received, when he bowed in enraptured humility before the masterpieces of Christian Art at the mysterious centre of the Church of the West. To secure something like this in his own home in far Northumbria he would not count the cost very closely.

Wilfrith's wealth

And if he did count the cost, he could meet it. Why the Commendatore should speak of the expense as being specially deterrent to him, I do not know. I see that among items under "Wilfrith" in the index of one of my books, there are "his magnificence" "his wealth." Indeed Eddi bases the hostile action of Ecgfrith's new wife, and of Ecgfrith himself, on these very points. She reminded the king of the secular pomp in which Wilfrith lived, and his wealth, and the number of his monasteries, and the magnitude of his buildings, and the innumerable army of attendants that he kept, royally clothed and armed. They plotted to destroy him, Eddi asserts, and seize his property. Money, we are told, had poured into his coffers. He could certainly afford to bring over master-workers in stone if he wanted them.

The great church at Ripon

Eddi, who knew if any one did know, puts the dedication of the great church at Ripon, which Rivoira would appear to have overlooked, before the building of Hexham. When I looked as carefully as I could into the probable date, I put it as "about 670 or 671." Nothing is said of who the artists were, the stone-carvers, the gold-workers, the weavers in purple and gold, the illuminators, the jewellers. The basilica was built of dressed stone, from the foundations in the ground to the top of the walls,

reared on manifold columns and porticoes. In its decoration gold and Splendour of Ripon
silver and purple were freely used. The altar was specially dedicated,
and its covering was of purple woven with gold. On the altar was a marvel
of beauty, the like of which—Wilfrith's chaplain tells us—had not been
heard of before in their times. This was a copy of the Gospels specially
prepared by Wilfrith's orders. He had not forgotten the impression made
upon him by his first visit to a church in Rome in the days of his early
youth. In the most prominent place on that altar was set a copy of the
Gospels, and he knelt down and prayed that he might be endued with
power from on high to teach the Gospel to the people. And now that
he had built a noble church in his own land, he was determined that the
Gospels should lie, in sumptuous form, in the same position. He ordered
that a copy should be prepared, written throughout in letters of the
purest gold on sheets of parchment coloured purple. For its cover he
ordered the metal-workers and the setters of jewels to make a case of pure
gold, richly adorned with most precious gems*. He clearly had already
collected a band of workmen, skilled to carry out anything which training
in Italy and France suggested to him as in accordance with the highest
tone of church art. So far as I know, nothing is said of foreign workmen
in this connection, though it would be to misunderstand the nature of a
chronicle of those times to found an argument on such an omission.

Rivoira speaks of the arts of building and carving having sunk to Art in the Heptarchy
a low ebb in the British Isles, as though the British Isles were at that time
one entity, of which a general statement could be made. His remark
presumably applied to England, with which we have to do. A much
more correct statement would be to the effect that as each kingdom of the
heptarchy adopted the new faith, building and carving and other arts
rose from the ashes to which the pagan English had reduced them, and
in some kingdoms rose so rapidly and to such heights that we have a right
to feel proud of our far-off ancestors. Take for example the country with
which we are at present specially concerned, Northumbria. Edwin, the
first Christian king, was baptised at York April 12, 627, in the Church of
St Peter the Apostle, which he had built of timber while he was being
catechised and prepared for baptism. As soon as he was baptised, he set

* Vitalian, who sent to us our Greek Archbishop Theodore, became Pope in 657. He was
in great favour at Constantinople, and the Emperor there sent him a book of the Gospels,
adorned with gold and precious stones, similar, we may suppose, to that which made such an
impression upon Wilfrith when he saw it on the altar at St Andrews, some four years before.
The art of these beautiful books, which we in England and the Scots in Hibernia carried to
a higher pitch of excellence than other races did, came to us, as Vitalian's book came to him,
from Byzantium, or through Byzantium.

Work of
Paulinus

to work to build a larger and more august basilica of stone, at the instigation of Paulinus, who of course was very familiar with the plan and structure of the churches at Rome where he had spent most of his life. The basilica was built four square, and it included within its walls the little oratory which Edwin had first constructed, and, as has now been discovered, the fountain of baptism. Before the walls had reached their full height, Edwin was slain in battle and Paulinus fled. The next Christian king, Oswald, made it his first business to complete Edwin's stone minster at York. The interposition of Paulinus may remind us of the many churches which Augustine's band of Romans built in Kent. Not later than 630, Paulinus, or his great convert Blaecca, built a remarkable stone church, *ecclesiam operis egregii de lapide fecit**, at Lincoln. The walls were still standing a hundred years after, in Bede's time, and indeed two hundred and fifty years after, in the time when the Ecclesiastical History was translated into Anglo-Saxon.

Aldhelm's
stone
churches

The early fervour of building churches of no mean type was not confined to Northumbria. Great stone churches were built by my predecessor Aldhelm of Malmesbury, in this same seventh century, which lasted hundreds of years. These churches were superior, J. R. Green says, quoting Freeman, to the famous churches Benet Biscop was rearing at this time by the Wear; not superior, the Northumbrian may reply, though he owe special allegiance to Aldhelm, to the churches Wilfrith was then rearing at Ripon and Hexham. Mr Green adds that Malmesbury and Sherborne were the only churches of that very early time—meaning, no doubt, the only large and important churches—which the Norman architects spared when the great rebuilding set in. Malmesbury was regarded by the Normans as a fitting church for a famous abbey, and it was only replaced by the present church about 1150. William of Malmesbury, who had then been dead a few years, evidently had not regarded a new church as necessary. Aldhelm's church at Sherborne served a line of 27 bishops as their seat, and was retained for monastic purposes after their time. As in the case of Ripon I have quoted a description of grandeur from a first-hand authority, so in the case of one of Aldhelm's churches I can quote Aldhelm himself. He composed a poem of 68 lines upon it; we would rather have had it in prose. "The house is resplendent with serene light, the sun shining through its windows of glass, and diffusing limpid light through the four-square temple. The golden pallia glow yellow with their woven threads, the fair clothing of the sacred altar. The golden chalice flashes with gems, as the heavens glow with blazing

* Bede, *H.E.* II. 16.

stars. There stands the broad paten, formed of silver, bearing the divine remedies of our life, for by the Body of Christ and his Sacred Blood are we fed. Here is the splendour of the Cross, with its plates of gold and silver adorned with gems. Here, too, the thurible, girt all round with capitals, hangs from on high, opening its perforations, through which the Sabæan incense shall breathe forth ambrosia when the priests are instructed to offer mass."

If space permitted, I should have liked to quote a charmingly poetic account which Aldhelm gives of the musical services in one of the other new basilicas.

While we have the accounts of the splendours of Ripon and Hexham told by Wilfrith's personal chaplain, and the splendours of Malmesbury told by Aldhelm himself, it may be as well to insert here the account of Biscop's pictures by Bede, who served under him and wrote his life. First, there were pictures of the ever-Virgin Mary, "the mother of God" in Bede's phrase, and the twelve Apostles, to stretch on boards from wall to wall in the nave. Then, pictures from the Gospel history for the south wall, and scenes from the Revelation for the north wall, in order that all who entered the church might see the ever lovable countenances of Christ and the Saints and so might dwell more intently upon the blessings of the Incarnation, or having before their eyes the perils of the last judgment might be led to examine themselves more closely*. That was in the church at Wearmouth. For the church at Jarrow he provided pictures shewing the connection of the Old and the New Testament. Thus Isaac bearing the wood for his own sacrifice and Christ carrying the Cross, were placed side by side; and the serpent raised up by Moses in the desert was illustrated by the Son of Man exalted on the cross. It may be noted that the setting forth of type and anti-type was a marked feature of the Eastern Church.

Another lesson of expansion of view beyond the narrowness of Rivoira's position is provided by the white marble altar at Bruton in Somerset. This altar was in one piece, with crosses sculptured all round its projecting edge. That is an apt description of the ancient altar slab of S. Satiro at Milan, whose enclosing screens both Aldhelm and Wilfrith and Birinus had no doubt seen. This great marble slab was brought over from Italy in the 7th century by Aldhelm, who gave it to his relative Ina, King of Wessex. Ina gave it to Bruton. William gives us its dimensions; they give a bulk of 13½ cubic feet. I asked a practical friend how many cubic feet of marble go to a ton. He replied, "of statuary marble, 13½ cubic

---

* See p. 49 on the feeling against burying on the north side of the church, to which Biscop's arrangement may have contributed.

feet." This may help to open people's eyes to the close relations between ecclesiastical Italy and England in the Wilfrith period. It may as well be added, as we have been discussing birds in scrolls, that Aldhelm's vestment which he wore when in Rome was still at Malmesbury in William's time. He tells us it was dyed scarlet and was ornamented with black scrolls containing the representations of peacocks.

Foreign
artists Again, there seems to be some confusion in Rivoira's idea of the position and work of the foreign artists said to have been introduced by Wilfrith. He writes—"Can we imagine that through mere contact with these foreigners, the rude local carvers attained the capacity for producing, with individuality of style, sculpture like that of Bewcastle and Ruthwell. Nothing short of a miracle could have accomplished that, and we should have to expect the previous growth of a national school, trained by the teaching of the foreign artists, and formed by the works they left behind them." And again, writing of Acca's cross, erected at Hexham on his death, he says, "is it likely that at Hexham in 740 a foreign sculptor should have been employed (for the author of what I, too, believe to be Acca's cross was clearly a foreigner) if Northumbria, as long ago as 671 already possessed the supposed school of artists capable of producing the Bewcastle and Ruthwell crosses." As far as I am concerned, the answer is simple. The foreign artists themselves of course came over to produce such exotic work as the Bewcastle and Ruthwell crosses, and no doubt much else that has disappeared. I never heard any other view. Mere contact with them would greatly stimulate any local carvers, and would tend towards the formation of a school of skilled carvers, the tone of the school being kept sound, for at least the times before the Danes came, by the works the foreigners left behind them, namely these very crosses.

The tomb-
stone of
Theodota Speaking as a Northumbrian, I do not at all see why one need postulate yet another foreigner for the one remaining of Acca's crosses. The little vine panel on the Bewcastle cross has in it the necessary germs. Two generations of loving Christian artists, inspired to beautiful developments of the art the foreigners left behind them, would quite account for the exquisite phenomenon. And we do not know what patterns the foreign artists of these crosses left as the treasures of the school. They certainly did not put all their patterns onto these two crosses; and of all conceivable patterns of theirs, surely none are more likely to have been freely developed than those composed of vine scrolls from Italy.

Rivoira finally suggests that the Acca Cross "may be due to some artist of the school of Ravenna, from which had issued not long before, about 720, the tomb of Theodota with its graceful vine sprays." But the vine sprays—so to call them—on this tomb, which is now at Pavia, are dullness and stiffness itself compared with the ivory chair at Ravenna, or compared with the Bewcastle Cross, a neighbour of Acca at Hexham. A distinguished man and most competent scholar like Rivoira must be very hard put to it for a loophole, when he credits the tombstone of Theodota with being the inspiration of Acca's lovely cross (Plate VI, 13), and flouts the inspiration of the cross hard by.

Of all men in the world the Commendatore Rivoira, the author of The Lombards the great Italian work on Lombardic Architecture, should credit the Northumbrian Angles with great power of initiative adaptation of lapidary types. The Lombards and the Angles were cradled side by side. The Lombards went south, the Angles went west. Harold of England was a Long-axe man to the end, witness the Bayeux Embroidery. If Alfred the Great, two centuries after the date with which we are concerned, chose the historical geography of Orosius as one of the four books he had put into Anglo-Saxon, that his people might know about their cousins in the land from which they themselves came, we may imagine it possible that Wilfrith and Biscop had in mind the ancient neighbourship between them and the Langobards. And considering the convulsions which at the time of their visit to Rome by way of Lombardy were afflicting the Lombard kingdom, the death of Rotharis in the year they started, the murder of Rodoald in the next year, the troubled reign of Aribert the church builder, the fraternal strife of his successors, we cannot but feel that there may have been some call of racial sympathy that would lead to an inflow of Lombard artists, seeking refuge from home troubles in a new and young and vigorous land, among people associated with their own ancestral home. And on the other hand we can well believe that they found in their adopted home in Northumbria the very same spirit of culture that had raised their own race to the architectural eminence which completed the great Church at Pavia four years before the Conference of Whitby.

We shall never understand the Anglian phenomena of the period Insulated under consideration until we have rid ourselves of insulated ideas. We ideas must abandon the short and narrow local view, and look far afield. The moment we do so, we see light. Take, for example, the time of Wilfrith. He was born in 634. On June 7, 632, Mahommed had died, after sweeping the Christians out of the countries between the Euphrates and the Red Sea. His successor swept them out of territories much nearer home. Above all others, I suppose, he made a clean sweep of people who produced works of art setting forth the history of Christ, and the representations in human form of Christ and the Apostles and the Saints. Who shall say where the wanderings of these artists towards the north-west came to an end? We have in our north-western islands the furthest point of the wanderings of the great red deer from their central home in the forests of Hungary and Bohemia. I do not at all think that we have in Northumbria an art decadent, shrunk, and enfeebled, as the red deer of our Scottish islands in comparison are. It would I think be more true to say, with a little of the exaggeration of that Eastern world to which I am claiming kinship in art, that the conditions of the known world towards the end of the seventh century, its tremendous explosions, were conspiring and combining to give us the power to produce the Ruthwell Cross, in honour of our own first religious poet. We ought never to forget that the fervour of Northumbria, in the development of the new culture, culminated less than a hundred years after Ruthwell in the greatest European scholar of his age, Alcuin of York.

I cannot quite understand some of Commendatore Rivoira's methods. He says (*Burlington Magazine*, XXI. 18 *n*. 29) that in my *Theodore and Wilfrith*, pp. 161, 162, I say "with all the air of certainty" that the Yarm stone is in memory of "Tunberht who was elected bishop of Hexham in 680 and deposed in 685, though such a date is mere guess-work as others too have seen." The name of the person whose memorial this is (Plate VI, 12) ends with the letters *mberchct*, and he is described as *sac*, that is, *sacerdos*. On this I remark at the place quoted, "In those early times *sacerdos* no doubt meant *bishop*; if not invariably, still so generally that it would be difficult to claim that here it means *priest* and not *bishop*. If it means *bishop*, no bishop except this one Trumbercht, ex-bishop of Hexham, had a name ending with these letters. The language is said to suit the date of our Trumbercht." "It seems very likely that we have here the actual tombstone of Trumbercht."

So much for my saying it with all the air of certainty. I make the likelihood depend on two points, the one, that *sac* means *sacerdos*, the other, that the language suits the period of Trumbercht. As for the date being guess-work, it seems to me to be arrived at by scientific method, and to be as free from guess-work as a rule-of-three sum, if the premises are correct, on which I specially do not express any approach to certainty.

But it would not have been worth while taking up your time with this small matter, if a much larger question was not involved. I deny that the opinion of a student closely trained in the investigation of these very questions, and full of experience, can be guess-work. Such a student could not make a mere guess if he tried to do so. All sorts of illustrative memories and comparisons crowd into his mind. A man of Commendatore

Rivoira's vast grasp and knowledge could not engage in mere guess-work Guess-work
on an important detail of Lombardic architecture. He may possibly
make mistakes when he deals with points not quite so familiar to him,
but even then it is not mere guess-work. We all of us are competent to
make mistakes; I offer myself as a palmary example of that competence,
and this present essay as an ideal opportunity for its display. But the
results, however regrettable, are not mere guess-work.

The opponents of the early date of these crosses have to get rid of the The Aber-corn Cross
great fragment at Abercorn, on which I lectured here twenty-seven years
ago*. It is reasonable to suppose that the cross was set up at the only
time when Abercorn was the seat of a bishopric, 681–685. Trumwine was
sent to minister to the Picts after their conquest by Ecgfrith, and he set
his bishop's seat at Abercorn, on the Northumbrian side of the Pictish
border. He naturally retired when the Picts slew Ecgfrith and recovered
their territories. The fragment which we possess presents remarkable
problems. Besides unusually beautiful foliage scrolls, it has three panels
of patterns, one being of simple and fairly good interlacement, the others
completely unlike anything at Bewcastle or Ruthwell, a good Chinese fret
and an elaborate dragon. These latter patterns are of course very often found
on the "Pictish" sculptured stones of Perthshire and Forfarshire. Thus
Bewcastle, Abercorn, and Ruthwell, provide us with almost every type
of the earliest post-Roman sculpture of these islands. If we ever found the
other pieces of the cross, what a revelation they would be.

The stone cross which Ethelwold, the ninth Bishop of Lindisfarne Ethelwold's Cross
(724–740), had made was so beautiful that the monks carried it about
with them in their wanderings. It was set up in the cemetery at Durham,
where it stood in the time of Symeon, soon after 1100. A beautifully
sculptured portion of a shaft taken from the walls of St Oswald's Church
is still to be seen at Durham; it is by tradition the cross of Ethelwold.
It belongs to the dragonesque and interlacement schools of art†.

Symeon of Durham gives us an interesting account of this cross.
Ethelwold became Bishop of Lindisfarne in 724 and held the bishopric
sixteen years. He ordered a stone cross to be embellished with skilful
ornamentation, and inscribed with his own name. This was duly carried
out. When the Danes sacked Lindisfarne they broke off the upper part.
An ingenious workman fastened it on again by means of melted lead. The
monks carried it about with them in all their wanderings after leaving
Lindisfarne, along with the body of St Cuthbert and his Gospel-book,

---

* See my *Theodore and Wilfrith*, pages 162–4, 225.
† *Theodore and Wilfrith*, pages 209, 293.

Ethelwold's Cross

the Northumbrians receiving the cross with great honour, out of their regard for both saints. Eventually it was set up in the cemetery at their new settlement, Durham, and there Symeon tells us "it stands sublime, telling the beholders of the memory of the two great men." The phrase *stans sublimis* does not indicate a cross of small dimensions. It is a pathetic picture, the train of monks dragging all over Northumbria from east to west and east again, besides all their personal belongings, the coffin of their patron and this great and beautiful specimen of the lapidary work of their school of art. They might well do this, for it was Ethelwold who supplied the illuminations for their noble Gospel-book. The cross has its art message for Professor Cook. It asks him to be just to a man who lived in the later part of the 7th century, was brought up in affectionate love for the art of his boyhood, and when he became a bishop determined to send down to posterity a voice that should tell of its fame. To be just to the monks, too, who at enormous personal cost were faithful to the purpose of their departed saint.

A general remark

One further general remark may be made on the Bewcastle and Ruthwell Crosses before we deal with details of their ornamentation.

As a great outburst in early times of a new style, due to some remarkable combination of new influences and new individualities, with new opportunities and new knowledge, I can understand them. As a late contradiction of national developments of subject, method, art, design, script, in a cultured lettered age, I cannot understand them. In the former aspect, I note a very large number of pre-Norman descendants, none quite equal to the parents, many coming very far indeed short of them. In the other aspect, I wonder how it is that there are no Plantagenet or Bruce descendants, when the things are so lovely in themselves, and Professor Cook and Commendatore Rivoira are scientifically certain that in that age there were artists who could turn out noble runic monuments of this rich order at the will of a patron.

CHAPTER III

Our Lord in Benediction.—Three branches of early art.—St Cuthbert's coffin.—St John Baptist.—The Ivory Chair of Ravenna.—The Annunciation and the Visitation.—The Flight into Egypt.—The Crucifixion.—The Bird.—Anglo-Saxon coins.—Paul and Antony.—Abbat Hadrian.—The Archer.—The lozenge-shaped O.—St Cuthbert's portable altar.—The dedication stone of St Paul's Jarrow.—The memorial of Ovin.—Acca's Cross.—The Chequers.—The Sundial.—The Falconer.—The Presence of Runes.—Pictish ornament.

We must now take into consideration some at least of the subjects Subjects on which we find on these two monuments. the Crosses

Supreme on each cross is the Figure of Our Lord. So far as I have Our Lord been able to ascertain, we have not evidence that other works of lapidary art of this high perfection were executed here, or indeed anywhere. It is probably not too much to say that in these figures of Our Lord at Bewcastle and Ruthwell we have the highest creations of a school of art with a long and continuous history behind it, tending always towards perfection and finding it here. The school had its beginning and its rise and its developments far in space from Northumbria and far in time from Alchfrith. By a happy concurrence of guiding forces its culmination sprang into life here. The power to represent in such calm majesty the human form of the Divine appears to have then passed away. We have not any examples of any early stages of decadence. The power was clean gone.

The school of artists remained; but having lost the consummate School of sculptor or sculptors, for I doubt if the artist was the same for the two artists crosses, the school devoted itself, with great success, on the one side to the representation of vine scrolls and vine interlacements, as on Acca's Cross, on the other side, and again with great success, to the development of complicated interlacements, as a parable of eternity, and to the convolutions of dragonesque creatures, so much less difficult to draw and to carve than living birds and semi-lacertine creatures of imagination, enjoying themselves on the tree of life. So far as art was concerned, there was no artistic reason why this latter branch should die out. There was endless variety and endless opportunity for the exercise of skill. As a matter of fact it not only did not die out, it lived a long and vigorous life in England, Scotland, and Ireland, and in many of its details it is exceedingly

Interlace- and rightly popular now, alike for sepulchral monuments and for personal
ments ornaments. I have intentionally kept clear of discussion, on this occasion,
of the complicated subject of interlacements. I have dealt with it so often
that it has become with me a subject too crowded with detail to be treated
as a side issue. It does not directly affect the date of the Ruthwell Cross.
In my judgment it does not affect the date of the Bewcastle Cross, for my
experience contradicts Rivoira's assertion that there are no interlacements
in this island until the 8th century.

St Cuth- Professor Cook contrasts the figures of Our Lord at Ruthwell with the
bert's coffin figure on St Cuthbert's coffin, of which he speaks very disparagingly. He
asks if it can be supposed that they belong to the same time and place.
We do not say that they do, so far as place is concerned. The figure in
the Washing of the Feet was carved in stone by a consummate artist.
The figure on the coffin was roughly grooved by a monk at Lindisfarne.
But if you leave the question of execution, on which the argument does
not depend, and compare the types, you will see a curiously real resemblance
between the two. I would rather maintain that they are taken from the
same design, with the great differences that grooving in wood and carving
in stone of necessity produce in a copy, than maintain that they are
absolutely diverse, and must be centuries apart.

It may be added that the figure of Alchfrith, perished as it has come
to be, is a remarkably bold and easy figure, with a graceful and appropriate
pose of active dignity. I do not know of any other representation of the
human form on an ancient monument in these islands which can compare
with it.

St John The combination of St John Baptist with Our Lord on the Bewcastle
Baptist shaft and on the Ruthwell Cross is the greatest link between the two
monuments. It is so striking as to be conclusive of interdependence,
especially when there are the further facts that the two monuments stand
alone in lapidary art in the extent and beauty of the continuous vine scroll
and in the amount of Anglian runic inscription found upon them.

The presence of the figure of Our Lord is natural at the date which we
assign to the monuments. The presence of the Baptist may be due to
the Eastern love for type and anti-type in connecting the old dispensation
with the new, the closing of the old and the opening of the new brought
together in sculpture as in the actual fact of their lives on earth. The
prominence assigned to the Baptist and to Baptism was very marked in
East and West alike. It was established in a very special manner at
Ravenna from the time of Galla Placidia. Maximian, the Archbishop

of Ravenna, selected the Baptist with the Lamb as the central figure on St John his magnificent *cathedra* of ivory (see Plate I), supported by the writers of Baptist the Gospels on either hand. This selection may have had a direct influence upon the selection of the Baptist as the only attendant Saint at Bewcastle and Ruthwell. In spite of this conclusive evidence of the early date of this subject, we find Professor Cook stating that the Baptist with the *Agnus Dei* "can hardly, according to the indications, be earlier than the 12th century." He quotes me (p. 285) as claiming that on the uprights on either side of the front of the chair we have the secret of the origin of the Bewcastle vine scrolls. His answer is, "Unfortunately for this theory it has been shown that the throne was not sent to Ravenna till the year 1001," as if it matters where the ancient chair was, so long as at its 6th century date it has the Baptist and the Lamb as its most prominent figure. The chair is fully dealt with in Chapter V.

The Annunciation and the Visitation, as found on the Ruthwell Cross, Annuncia-are taken by Professor Cook as evidences of late date. He finds them tion and Visitation represented in stone at some of the early French cathedral and abbey churches of the 12th century, and he regards these panels at Ruthwell as due to that influence, and of that date. Professor Baldwin Brown quotes a learned German who finds the Annunciation with a standing Mary in the primitive Syro-Palestinian type; and finds the Visitation on golden medallions from Adana at Constantinople of the 6th or 7th century, and on the 8th century altar of Ratchis at Cividale. It is also on Maximian's chair in the 6th century.

The Flight into Egypt Professor Cook says (p. 262) "is not known in Flight into Christian art till the 10th century at earliest, and does not appear in the Egypt monuments before the 11th century." Professor Baldwin Brown finds it on the medallions referred to above, in a form curiously like the Ruthwell form, with the tree that comes above the head of the ass. It was also on one of the lost tavolette of Maximian's chair.

The Crucifixion, Professor Cook says (p. 265), first appears in Roman The Cruci-painting in the 7th century. "It is rarely figured in sculpture in the fixion 10th century and does not become at all common till the 13th." It would be idle to dwell upon that argument; Ruthwell and Bewcastle attract us because they are uniquely uncommon. We have the Crucifixion on a 5th century ivory in the British Museum, slightly clad if at all, as at Ruthwell. As we have seen (p. 21) Biscop set up a representation of Our Lord on the Cross, *Filium hominis in cruce exaltatum*, in the Church of St Paul at Jarrow, to teach the lesson of type and anti-type.

A word or two may be said on the curious representation of a man and a bird on the top key of the cross-head at Ruthwell and the falconer and his falcon in the lowest panel at Bewcastle. Professor Lethaby has called my attention to representations of a similar character on Anglo-Saxon coins, shewn in Professor Baldwin Brown's great work on *The Arts of Early England* and Mr Keary's valuable treatise on *English Coins in the British Museum*. In the former book, vol. III, Plate VII, 1 and 2, there are two undated and unassigned sceattas with bird and man on the reverse, the bird in figure 1 being "charmingly wrought." This side of the coin is much worn, but it appears to have the same arrangement as the other coins referred to, namely, a bird on the left hand and a cross in the right hand of the man. Professor Baldwin Brown does not precisely decide that the two coins which he shews are Anglo-Saxon, but he regards England as the real home of the sceat currency, while allowing some measure of independent production in Holland. Mr Keary shews two undated Anglo-Saxon sceattas, vol. I, Plate II, figures 22 and 24, the king in each case with a cross in his right hand and a bird on his left hand, the bird replacing the second cross in the left hand which other coins shew. Mr Keary thinks that the bird replaces the Victory of the Roman coins copied by the Angles, as the long cross in the right hand replaces the Labarum. If it were not too minute for an essay of this character, something might be said of the possibility of some connection of the animal and decorative features of some of the earliest of the Anglo-Saxon coins with corresponding features of our two monuments.

While we are on the subject of coins, it may be well to mention a point which has a possible or not improbable bearing on the connection of Alchfrith with the runes on the Bewcastle shaft. We have several coins of Anglo-Saxon kings with the name of the king in runes. The earliest that I know are the coins of Peada (Pada) of Mercia and Ethelred of Mercia, two brothers who were kings 653–656 and 675–704 respectively*. Peada married Alchfrith's sister and became a Christian on Alchfrith's teaching and persuasion. Alchfrith married Peada's sister Cyniburga. The two young men were evidently close personal friends. Now of all the runic coins of Anglo-Saxon kings which I know of, one of the coins of Peada (Pada) stands out as having its runes perfectly cut, incomparably better than any of the others. And the beautiful runes for "Pada" are not at large on the field, they are contained in a very careful rectangular label. The "Æthelræd" of his brother's coins is very poor in comparison. It is clear that Alchfrith's brother-in-law and friend was a man of remarkable taste and art in the use of runes. He died fourteen years before the

---

* *The Arts of Early England*, vol. III, Plate IV, figures 1, 2, 3, 4.

memorial of Alchfrith was set up, but the recollection of his love for runic art may well have decided those who set it up to use the lettering which had been a source of interest and pleasure in the family circle, three of the surviving members of the family being recorded on the monument. I can even imagine the young men and women inventing the lapidary decorations of the runes for *g* and *k* as used at Bewcastle, of which something has to be said later on.

The bird in the top key of the cross, both with and without a man, Birds as surviving in full force without the man in the late Durham crosses, needs symbols further investigation than so far as I know has been bestowed upon it. The bird and man have a very marked history, in Christian story and in northern saga, in each case with a special English connection. The Christian story is, that on the death of the founder of the Church of the English, Pope Gregory, his memory was bitterly assailed in Rome, on the charge of wasting the treasures of the Church by lavish gifts to the poor for the purchase of personal popularity, and wanton destruction of the glories of art in Rome by the overthrowing of temples and the breaking up of statues. Peter the Deacon, that is, the Arch-deacon, in his zeal for Gregory, asserted in the pulpit that he had himself seen the Holy Ghost in the form of a dove whispering in Gregory's ear as he wrote*. Hence the mediaeval representation of Gregory with a bird at his shoulder. In the saga story, the bird, as shewn on the Leeds cross of King Onlaf, is the eagle, saying to its neighbour what a fool Sigurd is not to kill Regin while he sleeps, as Regin means to kill him and take the Fafner's treasure of gold as soon as he awakes. Apart from these connections, a bird at the ear or on the shoulder may usually be taken as a symbol of inspiration.

The one panel on the Ruthwell Cross which at first sight surprises us Paul and by its unexpectedness, is that which sets forth Paul and Antony, spoken Antony of as the first hermit and the first monk, breaking bread in the desert. Why should such a scene be found on this monument? David of Scotland had dispossessed the Culdees, who, if any class of churchmen, were followers of Paul and Antony. The occupants of the great abbeys which David founded were not at all likely to rule their manner of life after these African solitaries. Mr Cook finds a similar representation at Vézelay, attributed to the year 1135. He remarks that it is inconceivable that Ruthwell can have influenced Vézelay, which we may willingly allow, but adds that the influence of Vézelay may have been transmitted through one or another

* Peter died in the pulpit as he made this assertion. The common people, *varium et mutabile*, regarded this as a condign proof of the truth of the story and spared Gregory's library.

channel to Ruthwell. But why should either have affected or been affected by the other? To find two examples of two men breaking a circular cake of bread, in accordance with a story now commonly known, at two places so far remote from one another in those days—or indeed in these days—as Vézelay and Ruthwell, and to take it as a matter of course that one was related to the other, seems not very scientific.

Other examples It is not as if this subject had no other example in these islands. It occurs in a considerable number of cases in Ireland and in Scotland, on stones several of which are anterior to 1125. It is found in Ireland at Monasterboice and twice at Kells; and in Scotland at Nigg, Kirriemuir, and St Vigeans; to mention six examples which I have myself seen. Mr Cook disposes of them all by saying that they are much ruder than at Ruthwell. But what does that mean? That they were badly copied from Ruthwell, and that Ruthwell started the whole idea of Paul and Antony in Ireland and Scotland? Or does it mean that the subject was well known to the Celtic stone-cutters, and that David went out of his catholic way to take a very out-of-the-way subject from the Celtic repertory, because some one had drawn it better at Vézelay?

Why selected Can we suggest any special influence that should introduce the marked respect for these two African monks to this island? Indeed we can, and at the exact date which political considerations mark as probable for the sculpturing of this great monument. One of the most prominent ecclesiastics in England from about 671 onwards, indeed so far as teaching was concerned second only to our Greek Archbishop Theodore himself, was Hadrian, the Abbat of St Augustine's. He was the intimate friend, indeed the adviser specially appointed by the Pope, of Theodore, whose eastern training might need some such steadying influence. He had himself been pressed to take the archbishopric. Now Hadrian was an African monk, who had known about Paul and Antony from childhood. Contrast this influence upon Biscop and Wilfrith with any influence that can have affected David. It is not without significance that Paul and Antony are the two persons first named in Bede's Poetical Martyrology,

Deserti quartas primus capit accola Paulus,
Sedecimas Antonius obtinet atque Kalendas.

The Archer On the south face of the Ruthwell Cross the panel at the top of the shaft, which is in fact the lowest key of the cross itself, is occupied by an archer, aiming his arrow upwards to the right. He seems to be in a sitting position. There are many examples of archers, mostly very rude, on early Norman tympana, fonts, etc., and Professor Cook naturally finds examples on 12th century capitals etc. What is much more to the point is that we have in England several examples of archers on the shafts of The Archer great crosses of the pre-Norman type, in special connection with vine scrolls. I have shewn in my Disney Illustrations (1889, Pl. 2) examples of these at Auckland, Sheffield, Bakewell, and Bradbourne. The great shaft at Bradbourne, which I had taken out of a wall in many pieces and set up complete as far as it goes, has an archer at the foot of two of its faces. There is this great difference between these cases and that at Ruthwell, that while the Ruthwell archer is up at the very top, the other archers are at the very bottom and are evidently shooting at the birds, squirrels, etc., which are eating the fruits. The difference in idea is fundamental. Professor Cook remarks that "on the Ruthwell Cross, as well as on those at Bakewell and Bradbourne, the archers are aiming at the animals in the vines." The Ruthwell archer not only is not aiming at the vine scrolls, but he is above them and is aiming above himself, and indeed he is not even on the same side of the shaft with them.

I am of opinion that the archer on the Ruthwell Cross, aiming up at the cross-head in which he is, is placed there in connection with the remarkable statement in the runes of the poem inscribed on the cross, that the Lord of Heaven and Earth, fastened on the Cross, was "wounded with arrows." It may very well be that in course of time Christian sculptors combined the two features of this great work of early art, and in late Saxon or early Norman times put the archer at the bottom of the vine scrolls, and made his aim the animals and birds engaged in eating the fruit. There are two later examples of an archer shooting towards a Figure on the Cross, in each case in a locality where the Scandinavian legend of the death of Baldr, the demi-god of peace, may have had its influence, as it conceivably had with the author of the *Dream of the Holy Rood* whose main elements appear in the Ruthwell runes. Baldr was so great a favourite with the demi-gods of Asgard that an oath was taken from all the trees that they would never harm him. It became a sport to hurl wooden javelins and shoot wooden arrows at him. They never hurt him. But it occurred to the clever Loki, the spirit of mischief, that the oath was not proffered to the mistletoe, as not being a tree, and yet there was substance enough in an old bush of mistletoe to make a fatal point to an arrow. He constructed the weapon and one of the demi-gods shot it at Baldr and killed him.

Something must be said of the form of letters in the Latin inscriptions Palaeo- on the Ruthwell Cross, some portions of which are shewn in figure *a* graphy on page 3.

One of our best ascertained relics of the date to which we attribute the cross of Alchfrith is the portable altar found on the breast of St Cuthbert

St Cuthbert's altar

in 1827*. It is a small piece of black oak, thin, covered with plates of embossed silver. This is not the occasion to describe embossed patterns and inscriptions. Cuthbert, who was a youth in 651, died in 687, two years after the Picts cast off their short subjugation by King Ecgfrith. The art and the inscriptions of the silver plate are clearly of that time or earlier, and of the "Kentish" type of ornaments from excavations. It is of importance to note that they suggest a Greek origin, if indeed the inscription is not itself Greek as was the case with the cross found in the 11th century on the breast of Acca of Hexham, the intimate friend of Bede. Acca died in 740.

But early as the silver plates are, the little slab of oak which they cover is older still. It has itself been a portable altar. There are incised on it two crosses and the legend *in honor...S. Petru,* dating from a time and place at which the Greek genitive of St Peter was used instead of the Latin. It would be difficult to find the lozenge-shaped O more beautifully cut than in this word *honor.* No one can say how early this local example is.

Jarrow dedication

Another local example is specially interesting, for it seems to shew a point of transition. The Church of St Paul at Jarrow was consecrated in the 15th year of King Ecgfrith (685). We have the dedication stone, with a full inscription in Latin, Plate VII, 14. The capital O occurs eight times. In four cases it is a rounded oval, in three it is a good lozenge, in one it is half-and-half. The word *conditore* has in it one of the best examples of each class; a useful warning against building much argument as to date on a point like this. It is scarcely necessary to adduce the initial pages of the Gospels in the Lindisfarne Book, where both kinds of O are used†.

The Ruthwell use is closely in accordance with the contemporary use at Jarrow. While in the example which I give of the use of the lozenge-shaped O there is no oval O, both of the O's in the word *cognoverunt* at another part of the inscription are oval.

Lozenge-shaped O

Professor Cook finds the lozenge-shaped O at Nonantola near Modena, carved in 1117, and at Piacenza, carved about 1122, and these he cites as favourable to his Davidian theory. It would have been better if he could have cited local use in his favour, as I have in my favour. At so late a period as 1128, the influence of a princely builder of Abbey Churches and erector of noble crosses exquisitely carved, covered with archaic runes, and one of them covered with Latin inscriptions in beautiful letters of palaeological script, should have provided him with a fair number of parallel examples elsewhere in the border lands, in lapidary inscriptions.

* *Theodore and Wilfrith,* p. 105.

† In the book of Kells, in two cases a half O is used, like a thin capital D.

But even if such were forthcoming, they would not be any argument against our date for Ruthwell, fortified as we are with contemporary local examples. Professor Cook does not say that M and G exist at Nonantola in the Ruthwell form. Without that evidence, the lozenge O has no weight in this case.

Professor Lethaby has worked out the alphabet of the Ruthwell inscriptions, and his scientific results completely support my results of nearly thirty years ago as shewn in the figure on page 3. The special uncials, such as M, are of the early Scoto-Northumbrian type. The G also is a typical letter, as used in place of the J of *Jacobi* on the Hawkswell Cross. Professor Cook (p. 249) does not appear to have understood my remarks on this Hawkswell G, or to have realised the datal importance of the form of the faded inscription, *Haec est crux sancti Jacobi.*

We have another Latin inscription which is probably not much later than this at Jarrow, the memorial of Ovin; it may even be a little earlier.

In connection with Ecgfrith's first marriage, with Etheldreda the widow of a prince of the Gyrvii from whom she received Ely as a marriage gift, we have an interesting monument still remaining. Twelve years after the marriage, Etheldreda left him and returned to Ely, the conjugal life having been specially distasteful to her. It is understood that Wilfrith took her part, and that this caused his first breach with the king*. Etheldreda had brought with her a monk-steward, one Ouini, of whom Bede (*H.E.* iv. 3) gives a very loving account. He went, later, to Lastingham. At Haddenham, one of Etheldreda's chief manors, there was found the base or socket stone of a cross, with a portion of the cross-shaft itself. On the base, in uncials which may well be of the later 7th century, is the inscription, *Lucem tuam Ovino da Deus et requiem. Amen.* This interesting relic of Etheldreda's time now stands in the south aisle of the Church of Ely.

A comparison of the forms of letters in the Jarrow inscription and the Ovin inscription, which the kindness of the Dean of Ely has enabled me to make, has interesting results. The Q is the same in the two cases, the circumference being not broken by the mark attached. E, C, A, O, are the only letters which shew differences. The E at Ely is in all six cases round; at Jarrow it is in nine cases square, only once round. The one C at Ely is round; at Jarrow it is round in seven cases, square in one. The opposite treatment of E and C at Jarrow nearly corresponds to our modern treatment. The A at Ely has the cross line straight in all four cases; at Jarrow it is only once straight. The O at Ely is in

Ovin's monument

* See my *Theodore and Wilfrith*, pages 127, 128.

both cases round; at Jarrow, as we have seen, it is in four cases round in three cases a lozenge, in one case half-and-half. It is satisfactory to find these close resemblances in two memorials, the one of 685 the other but little later, inscribed at places far apart, but significant of the fact that Ecgfrith was Etheldreda's husband and Ovin was her steward.

What the Ruthwell Cross is not So far as art, or language, or substance of language, is concerned, Ruthwell is nothing, has nothing, of all of the much it might in that position in that 12th century have had or been. It is not Scottish or Pictish, i.e. has nothing in common with the almost countless remains of art of the Argyllshire or the Forfarshire styles which were abundant at that time. It is not Norman, it is not French. It is not 12th century English in language or in substance of language. It is not Irish, it is not any kind of Celtic, it is emphatically not Norse. It has in its runes no leanings towards the many departures from Greek forms of letters which by that time had set in in full swing. In fact, it is unique. And therefore, a certain school of archaeology says, it is late, because, being unique, we have not any early example of it. We might reply that as we have no late example of it, it is therefore early. But neither argument is worth stating.

We may now turn to the Bewcastle Cross.

Acca's Cross In regard to Acca's Cross Rivoira says, "As a matter of fact, the carving on the Acca fragments, consisting of pairs of vines coiled in circles with interlacing sprays carved with leaves and grapes, is so different in composition, design and execution from the Bewcastle and Ruthwell scroll-work, that any idea that they are products of the same school is out of the question." The lowest panel but one, on the south side of the Bewcastle Cross, is a direct contradiction of this assertion. We have there all the elements out of which the decoration of Acca's Cross was developed by natural process. See Plates V, 7, VI, 13.

A word or two should be said on one panel of the Bewcastle Cross of which much has been said. It is not worth many words. Sir Martin Conway has settled the question*.

In the year following the publication of his book, Professor Cook published a useful series of "accounts of the Bewcastle Cross," beginning with Roscarrock (1607) and Camden (1607). In the preface he points out, as "sufficiently curious to be remarked," "that the first two persons that

---

* Sir Martin Conway has shewn (*Burl. Mag.* XXIV. 85–9) that we have the checks as ornaments on gold pendants of the 7th century, one from Sibertswold, another at Sarre. St Eloi's golden chalice at Chelles, destroyed at the French Revolution, was covered with checks.

deal with the cross refer it to the twelfth century." But they only do this ^{The} indirectly, by supposing the large panel of chequers to represent the arms ^{chequers} of the de Vallibus family, or Vaux, of Gilsland, the local magnates. Professor Cook tells us that Hubert de Vallibus received the barony of Gilsland from Henry II in 1158*, five years after the death of David I, who, according to Professor Cook, erected the cross. The two views that the chequers are the Vaux arms and that David erected the cross are mutually destructive, and it is only because they were taken to be the Vaux arms that these two earliest writers can be said to have dated the shaft in the twelfth century.

The chequers are of course not meant for armorial bearings at all. To suggest that they are is as much out of the question as it would be to suggest that the archer on the Northumbrian shaft now at Ruthwell was placed there because Nigel de Albini, to whom the lands of the forfeited Mowbray Earl of Northumberland were given, was bow bearer† to William Rufus and Henry I. Chequers are an attractive ornament on a small shrine of wood or metal. A thin plate of silver has alternate squares cut out of it, and is then fixed on the side of the shrine, the colour of which shews through the squares cut in the plate of silver, and a very ornamental effect is produced. An Irish shrine thus adorned is in existence. The effect is admirably reproduced on the Bewcastle shaft.

In the sun-dial Professor Cook finds evidence of late date. "According ^{The} to Gatty," he says, "few sun-dials in England antedate 1066. Collingwood, ^{sun-dial} who lists several in Cumberland, will not assert that any of them were sculptured before the Norman period." He adds on his own account, "It will be seen that there is absolutely no reason for dating the Bewcastle sun-dial earlier than the late 11th century, and that the 12th century is more probable." In answer to this it has been noted that there is a Roman sun-dial in the museum at Corbridge, and that the sun-dial on the ancient Saxon church of Escomb, near Bishop Auckland, with fragments of Roman inscriptions in its walls, is apparently original. Professor Cook has a description of the Bewcastle dial as divided by the radii into twelve divisions between sunrise and sunset. In dealing with dials that is a point of high importance.

I shew in Plate VII, 17, a sun-dial made in Anglo-Saxon times, when Edward the Confessor was king, and Tostig was earl of Northumbria. It is at the church of Kirkdale, near the moors on which Lastingham lies, and not far from Bransdale, the dale presumably of Brand. The church

---

* The Historic Peerage does not quite agree with this.
† Register of Furness Abbey.

has priceless remains of the earliest Anglian and Scotic work. We may take this very careful dial as an example of what a Northumbrian dial of the 11th century was like. Anything more unlike Bewcastle it would be difficult to imagine. It is divided by the radii into eight divisions, with special marks at four of the hours, the most important liturgically being marked with a cross. Above all, it tells us what the language and script of the period in Northumbria was in the 11th century. The language is so like our speech of to-day that you do not need to know a word of what we call Anglo-Saxon to understand it all, unless it be the word *dagum* for 'days,' which any one could guess. If the good men Haward and Brand had desired to shew that their work and talk were centuries newer than the work and talk of the Bewcastle sculptor, they could scarcely have made it clearer. As for runes, they used the two which then survived in common use in Anglo-Saxon, the runes for *w* and *th*; how hopelessly unlike this a monument is which professes according to Professor Cook to be sixty years later and has nothing but runes, it is unnecessary to point out.

Professor Cook does not appear to have formed a correct estimate of the references to hawks and falcons which he finds in early times. His remarks have created some difficulty in some quarters, as though it was a very unlikely thing that hawking was so well known in England in 670 that a king should be represented on his funeral monument with a hooded falcon. There were plenty of Roman tombstones in the region of the Roman Wall, and the idea of representing on the tombstone something personal to the dead man or woman was not absent from these memorials. If the prince who was commemorated was more than ordinarily interested in hawking, either as a sport or more probably as the means of procuring the savoury meat his soul loved, it would be very natural to represent him with his falcon, especially if the use of the falcon or hawk was not as yet common.

When I was writing my *Boniface of Crediton*, I came to the conclusion that the references to hawks and falcons within seventy or eighty years of 670 amounted to a justification of the early date of the Bewcastle panel. Professor Cook allows that hawks for hawking purposes must have been comparatively numerous on the continent, as they are mentioned in Germanic laws from the 5th to the 7th century. It is too much to assume that they were unknown in this island in the latter part of the 7th century, which is what Professor Cook's argument amounts to in the end. There is much more point in the view that they were presumably known and used here, if they were common on the continent.

In 742 the English missionary bishop of Germany, Boniface of Evidence of Boniface Crediton, persuaded Karloman of Austrasia to hold a Council for the abatement of abuses*, which were many and grievous. It was the first Council of its kind in that period. Only the more common abuses were dealt with on such an occasion. The acts and decrees are not numbered; the fourth in order deals with the manner of life of priests. They are forbidden to carry arms, or to fight, or to go with the army unless specially appointed to act as chaplains, for a full supply of whom careful arrangement was made. Hunting and wandering in the woods with dogs was equally forbidden to all ministers of God, "and we have forbidden them to have hawks or falcons." Hawking must, therefore, have been quite common in that time, as a means of obtaining food in the first instance.

As to the practice of hawking in England, Professor Cook would have us regard the English of the time as far behind the people of the Continent; why, I do not know. He quotes a letter of Boniface to Ethelwald king King Ethelwald of Mercia as somewhere between 732 and 754. We can come nearer to its date than that. Boniface wrote two letters to Ethelbald, one a very pleasant letter, the other very much indeed the reverse. This second letter, a terrible indictment, is dated 745–6. It is clear that the other was the earlier of the two. It should be noted that Ethelbald was only the next generation below his relative Cyniburg, the wife of Alchfrith of the Bewcastle Cross. In this earlier letter we read†, "In token of our true love and devoted friendship we send to you a hawk, two falcons, two shields, and two lances. These small gifts we beg you to receive, unworthy as they are." There was certainly nothing unusual in the passage of falcons to England or in their use there, in the generation next below Alchfrith.

Professor Cook refers to another of the long series of Bonifatian letters, King Ethelbert the letter of Ethelbert II of Kent to Boniface. Ethelbert's grandfather was reigning when the Bewcastle Cross was erected. Professor Cook misunderstands the letter, as shewing that "even in the middle of the 8th century there were very few trained hawks in Kent." Its evidence is quite in the opposite direction‡. "One thing more I desire you to do for me. From information received, I do not at all think it will be a matter of much difficulty to you. It is, to send me a pair of falcons, whose bold nature it is to be keen to catch and strike herons and bring them to the ground. The reason for my asking you to obtain and send me these birds is, that very few hawks are found in Kent which breed such good birds, active, and fierce, that can be tamed and trained and

---

* *Boniface of Crediton*, p. 182.　　　† *Boniface of Crediton*, p. 241.
‡ *Boniface of Crediton*, p. 235.

taught for the above-mentioned purpose." Clearly there was plenty of hawking in Kent for birds less powerfully armed for defence than the heron is, and more suitable for the table. Failing other evidence, the falcon was not an anachronism late in the 7th century, if it was so much used here in the middle of the 8th.

Alfred's falcons

The importance of hunting and hawking as means of obtaining food must have been very great, indeed paramount. A hundred years later than Ethelbert we are told that Alfred had these arts in perfection, and personally trained and worked his hounds, and taught his falconers hawkers and kennel-men their business. The necessity was presumably greater at the much earlier stage of civilisation in Alchfrith's time. The science of hawking may well have been with Alchfrith, as it was with Alfred, a specially valuable accomplishment and a source of proper pride; worthy of note on his sepulchral monument.

Why should David use runes?

I have not seen anything that can be called an attempt to explain why David, either as a Normanising noble holding an English earldom in the twelfth century, or as the representative in line of the Celtic kings of Scotland, or as the son of a thoroughly reforming churchwoman, should cover his monuments with Anglian runes, which were no longer the script of the English and never had been the script of the Normans or of the Scots. If it was done by him as a compliment to the English people who might see the crosses, I fear that archaeology had not in that age come sufficiently into its own to make the compliment strike home. But indeed the suggestion of such a compliment, under the depressed conditions of the Anglo-Saxons and under the jealousy of the watchful dominant Norman, scarcely deserves attention. And I am sorry to feel obliged to add that Professor Cook's answer that runic inscriptions were in use then, as evidenced by runes at Pennington, Carlisle, Bridekirk, and elsewhere, has nothing whatever to do with the runes of the early Anglian *futhorc* in use at Bewcastle and Ruthwell. The few queer runes to which he points could many of them not be read by one who knew only, however well, the runes on those monuments, while their language has nothing to do with the language on the crosses. The argument amounts to a confession that there is nothing to be said in support of the presence of these largest collections of Anglian runic letters at any such date as 1125.

Pictish ornamentation

The intercourse between the Northumbrians and their northern neighbours the Picts of Caledonia was at some periods close. When Edwin of Deira conquered his Bernician rival Ethelfrith, the sons of the defeated king fled northwards. Oswald made his way westward to Iona, and this led to the establishment of the Scotic Church in Northumbria.

Eanfrith stayed among the Picts and married the daughter of their king. As the descent of the kingship was by mother-right in Pictland, their son Talorgan became king of the Picts, his patronymic being Mac Ainfrith. He was Oswy's nephew, and first cousin to Ecgfrith, Alchfrith, and Aldfrith, but he died early, in 656. Ecgfrith conquered the Picts, but was eventually killed in battle with them near Forfar in 685.

It would be natural to suppose that the Northumbrian Angles learned **Pictish** from their neighbours some of the traditional skill of the Picts in drawing **patterns** figures of animals, and various patterns curiously akin to early work at Mycenæ. As long ago as Stilicho's invasion of Caledonia (A.D. 399), the poet Claudian, who was in Stilicho's retinue, describes the Roman soldier pausing in the fight to wonder at the drawings or paintings on the body of his stricken foe.

Perlegit exsangues Picto moriente figuras.

These same drawings, probably done with stencil plates, were according to my theory transferred to memorial and boundary stones when the Christian teachers persuaded the Picts to partially cover their bodies with clothes. Judging from the remarkable examples of such stones as still exist, it may well have been that the dragonesque school of Northumbrian art, and the school which dealt with interlacements, had some connection with the contemporary art of Pictland.

On the other hand, I feel that we must trace some of the more classical **Bede and** examples of surface ornament in Pictland, such as we find at St Vigeans **the Picts** near Arbroath, to direct communication with Northumbria at the period with which we are dealing. We find that in 710 Naiton, King of the Picts, sent messengers to Abbat Ceolfrid of Wearmouth and Jarrow, begging that he would write for him a treatise on the true computation of Easter, and would send him architects to build a church after the Roman manner. The treatise, which no doubt Bede himself wrote, occupies thirteen closely printed octavo pages in Latin. The architects were sent, and it was presumably through them that some of the classical scrolls got a footing at ecclesiastical centres of the Picts.

CHAPTER IV

The date of the Ruthwell Cross.—Wide differences between it and the Bewcastle shaft.—The Nimbus.—Didron and Professor Cook.—The Robes of Our Lord.—The Beard.—Wilfrith's journeymen.—Crosses and Altars.—Ancient churchyards.—Triple crosses.—Paulinus.—Antecedent improbability.—Late remains at Durham.—Their bearing on the theories of Cook and Rivoira.—The Caedmon and Bede Crosses.

Date of the Ruthwell Cross

Professor Cook is kind enough to quote frequently from some of my fairly numerous little books on our earliest Church History. He represents my opinion on the date of the Ruthwell Cross thus*.—"George F. Browne † was confident that the Ruthwell Cross was erected before the death of King Ecgfrith in 685." But the statement to which he gives the reference in my *Theodore and Wilfrith* has not that meaning. It is as follows:— "After his [Ecgfrith's] defeat and death in 685, the Britons and Picts in that corner of what is now Scotland, as also the Picts in Fife, resumed the native sway, and the Angles were known there no more. There has been no other period in history when a great Anglian Cross, covered with Anglian runes, could have been set up in that south-western district of Scotland. Tradition points to its being regarded by the inhabitants as of foreign [that is, not Scottish] origin, not native. It was brought, they say, by sea, from distant parts, and was for a time at Priestwood-side, near the sea. It was being brought inland: but the hauling gear failed, and the people took that as an indication that it must remain on the spot which it had reached. They put a shed over it, and the place became known as Rood-well." My position is that if it was created for erection at Ruthwell, no period but that of Ecgfrith fulfils the conditions. But the tradition is that it was not originally meant to be set up there.

Local tradition

In a long experience of investigations in these islands and elsewhere, I have learned not to disregard local traditions. Who first invented, out of nothing that ever happened, the nucleus of that tradition?—that is the question which I put to myself, and have often put to others. The traditions are there, who put them there? This story of the arrival of the Ruthwell Cross on the south coast of what is now called Dumfries is certainly in its main features of early date, for the Ruthwell Cross has for long had a known history. It stood in the Church of Ruthwell before the Reformation, and was an object of so much veneration that it was

* Page 224.　　　　† *Theodore and Wilfrith*, p. 236.

not disturbed when the Reformation came with all its vandalism. The
Cross held its own till 1642, when, on July 21, the general Assembly of the
Church in Scotland ordered its destruction, on the ground that its existence
tended to idolatry. It was thrown down in the church and broken into
three or four pieces, which were left in the church for eighty years or
more, and were then turned out into the churchyard.

With this preface, I may pass to the consideration of striking differences
between the Cross at Ruthwell and the shaft at Bewcastle.

"Modern writers," Professor Cook says*, "are practically unanimous
in assuming that they belong to the same period and school. Postulating
this, we have only one problem to solve in our attempt to date the two
crosses."

I am far from thinking that it is so simple as to be only one problem.
With all my realisation of the immense strides in the application of art to the
Christian story in the time of Biscop and Wilfrith, I have a definite feeling
of wonder as to whether there was time between 670 and 685 for changes
so great as from Bewcastle to Ruthwell. One easement of the difficulty
comes from the fact that the earlier of the two is a sepulchral monument,
while the later is of the nature of a "teaching cross," setting forth details
of the Christian story. It is probably unnecessary for me to point out
that the difficulty which I feel is largely increased when I am asked to
regard these two crosses, with their extremely diverse characteristics,
as put up by one and the same man with one and the same purpose.
I might add, also, that differences might pass with slight notice in 670 and
685 which would cry out for notice and disapproval at a period when
ecclesiastical and secular decorative arts had reached so high a point as
in the days of David's brother-in-law and friend, King Henry the Beauclerc.

I will take, for the present, one point of difference between the two.
Curiously enough, Professor Cook himself states† that it is essential, a
remarkable comment on his theory of the same period (A.D. 1125)‡ and
school. At Bewcastle, and next to each other on the same face of the
shaft, our Lord has the nimbus, the Baptist has not. At Ruthwell, in
the same contiguity, each figure has a nimbus. I must point out in passing
that this is to my mind a clear indication of a date at which there were
vague ideas about the use of the nimbus, and there was no settled practice.

Whole volumes could be written on the subject of the nimbus.
Mr Cook quotes from Miss Stokes's translation of Didron as follows§:

* p. 218.　　　　　　　　† pp. 236, 237.
‡ I take 1125 as a mean date. Some of Professor Cook's illustrations from French cathedrals
make that early rather than late.　　　§ p. 258.

The Nimbus "The nimbus is not constantly figured around the head of saints, in monuments belonging to a period earlier than the 11th century," and there he stops, fatal as the quotation is to an absence of the nimbus in the 12th century. But Didron continues thus, in Miss Stokes's translation*:

"The Christian nimbus is not found on well authenticated monuments anterior to the sixth century. The transition from the complete absence to the constant presence of the nimbus was effected during the seventh, eighth, and ninth centuries. During that period, figures even on the same monument are represented sometimes with and sometimes without that attribute." That is even more fatal to a 12th century example.

It is evident that when Miss Stokes represents Didron as saying that the nimbus is not constantly figured earlier than the 11th century she is taking "constantly" from an original *constamment*. To make sure I consulted the French text (Paris, 1853) and I found that Didron's word is *constamment*. Littré gives only two meanings for this word, 1. *Avec constance*, 2. *Invariablement*. As this is not a case of martyrdom, the only meaning is "invariably." That is to say, Didron, in the part which Professor Cook quotes as his witness, authoritatively, makes the use of the nimbus invariable from the 11th century, and thus rejects Professor Cook's claim that David erected the Bewcastle Cross fairly well on in the 12th century. And in the part which he does not quote, Didron places the Bewcastle Cross in the seventh, eighth or ninth century, in which periods figures of saints even on the same monument appear sometimes with and sometimes without the nimbus.

If Didron is to be taken as authoritative—and it is to be noted that he is full of knowledge of the French Cathedrals from the point of view of Christian Art, and refers 21 times to Reims and 49 times to Professor Cook's favourite storehouse Chartres—what can be said in defence of the Davidian theory? On a point of such vital importance as the absence of a nimbus on the head of John the Baptist while on the same stone and actually on the same face of the stone there are two cases of the presence of the nimbus, David for some reason flew in the face of the very influence to which Professor Cook assigns the existence of the Bewcastle Cross. That David was completely ignorant on the point, and merely blundered badly, to the extent of harking back a couple of centuries or more to what he would regard as a barbarous period, is a view that would displace him from the position on which Professor Cook's claim for him depends. To assert that his artist learned better before the Ruthwell Cross was carved, is to hang the whole of Mr Cook's plea on

* *Christian Iconography*, i. 99.

a very slender peg, and Didron directly condemns that explanation. Didron's words as they stand are completely in accordance with the date which I prefer to Mr Cook's date.   If any one wishes to have before him two completely dissimilar figures of the Baptist, let him set side by side the Bewcastle figure and the figure at the supposed source of David's inspiration, the Cathedral Church of Chartres.

I may add that Our Lord's nimbus on the Ruthwell Cross, where it occurs three times, is much larger and more prominent than at Bewcastle. Also, it differs in having three parallel lines, horizontal, proceeding from behind the head on each side, where the ends of the arms of a Cross are shewn in the so-called Cruciform nimbus, and three vertical lines above the head.   These clearly marked rays are in my judgment much more early than late in their tone, as, again in my judgment, the absence of any such mark at Bewcastle is a sign rather of early than of late date.   The large size of the nimbus at Ruthwell is specially noteworthy.   In Professor Cook's figure 12, which shews the figure of the Baptist and the head of the Lord in the panel below, the small size and the flatness of the Baptist's nimbus are in very startling contrast with the Lord's nimbus below.   Indeed any one looking at the Ruthwell Cross as there shewn, and as I have seen it, must allow that there is something to be said for the suggestion I made* many years ago.   "It seems not impossible that this upper part, about five feet six inches high, was the original cross, and the great shaft, twelve feet high, was a few years later."   We have plenty of examples of crosses socketed on to shafts; indeed I do not doubt that Bewcastle itself is a contemporary example.

The robes of Our Lord shew marked differences on the Ruthwell Cross.   The clothing in the Feet-washing panel is quite unlike the clothing in the other two panels and quite unlike that at Bewcastle.   Curiously enough it is in remarkable agreement with the robing of the figure of Christ incised on the coffin of St Cuthbert, who died two years after the defeat and death of Ecgfrith in 685 restored the parts now called Dumfries-shire to Scotland.   It may be noted in passing that the rudeness of these incised lines is turned to unscientific use by Professor Cook.   He contrasts it, as an evidence of the art in Northumbria towards the end of the 7th century, with the beauty of the sculpture of Our Lord's Figure on the two crosses.   It is enough to say in reply that the monks of Lindisfarne grooved the lines on the coffin as well as they could from some design closely resembling the one referred to at Ruthwell, while some consummate

* *Conversion of the Heptarchy*, p. 206.

lapidary sculptor wrought the figure on the Cross*.   The robes at Bewcastle are markedly different from any of those at Ruthwell, especially in the pleating of the under garment.

The clothing of the Baptist at Bewcastle is not unlike that of Our Lord immediately below.   At Ruthwell it is rude and rough, clumsy in the parts that are not broken away.   This is another indication in the direction suggested in a previous paragraph.

Sca Maria at York   While I am speaking of the beauty of the sculptured figures and robes of Our Lord on these crosses in the north, I must take note of the most beautiful sculpture of this character that I have ever seen, the noble Madonna and Child recently unwalled in York Minster by Mr Eric Maclagan. A cast of it can be seen at the Victoria and Albert Museum.   It is as fresh as if it was still in the artist's studio.   There is a perfectly cut S ꓑ A, and the final *a* in Maria' is of the type of the *a* in the great Wearmouth Pandect of the end of the century we have under consideration, several of the leaves of which are now known in addition to the one recognised and rescued some years ago by the great benefactor of archaeologists, W. Greenwell of Durham.

The Beard   Another example of development is even more striking.   At Bewcastle Our Lord is beardless, at Ruthwell, bearded.   It seems unreasonable to suppose that King David, who was getting his patterns from Chartres and other highly developed places, should actually hark back to the earliest times, when a Saint's nimbus was as likely as not to be absent, and when Our Lord was beardless.   The arrangement of the hair also differs on the two crosses.   Such differences are natural in an early creative period; they are very hard to explain away in the middle of the 12th century.

However you may look at these striking differences, one fact stands out clear, namely, that to make dogmatic assertions of date upon such foundations, on the assumption that at a given early date the Christian artists in all parts of the West were producing the same designs, treating details in the same way, is consonant neither with reason nor with evidence.

But that limitation to "the West" is the rock on which much of the special pleading against the early date of these two great monuments is wrecked.   The East was more inventive than the West.   Both at Bewcastle and at Ruthwell we have the hand of the East.   The hand of the East was dominant in many parts of Italy when Wilfrith and Biscop learned the root principles of Christian Art.   The Church at Rome had been a Greek-

* There is a striking similarity between the robes of this design, the book, and the nimbus, and the corresponding details of an early figure in the Museum at Ravenna.   See Conway, *Burl. Mag.* XXIV. 86.

speaking church at the beginning. The Scriptures and the Liturgy were afterwards put into Latin because it was the vulgar tongue of Rome. Many of the early Popes were Greeks. We have seen that the Mahommedan successes drove the Christian artists westward. The same was the case with the Greek scholars and theologians. In such numbers did the learned Greeks come from Constantinople to Rome when the Mahommedan tents covered the opposite side of the Bosphorus, and so important were they, that the twelfth Pope from Vitalian, who sent the Greek Theodore to Canterbury, was the seventh Greek in succession who had been made Bishop of Rome. It will be remembered that when Constantinople was taken in 1453, the flight of Greek scholars westward restored the knowledge of their language to western Europe and was thus the prelude of the Reformation. Eastern influence

Besides these minuter but very serious differences in detail, there is the obvious difference that the two monuments are as unlike each other in their general treatment as two ancient monuments can well be. There is no interlacement at Ruthwell; at Bewcastle it is a marked feature. There is no Latin inscription at Bewcastle; at Ruthwell it is a marked feature. Two of the faces at Bewcastle are broken up into a number of disconnected panels with no apparent meaning beyond that of the occupation of surface with ornamentation of divers kinds. There is no approach to that at Ruthwell. General treatment different

But when we look for the essential difference, we find it in the memorial figure of the man with the falcon. No matter who the man may be, that panel marks off the Bewcastle Cross from the Ruthwell Cross by a vital difference, as the scene panels mark off the Ruthwell Cross from the Bewcastle Cross. If they are the work of one mind at one period, that mind was astonishingly fertile, and open to curiously diverse inspirations.

It may be well to say something in detail upon the work done by Wilfrith's band of skilled workmen, moving about from place to place in Mercia while he was being kept out of his Northumbrian see, and doing church work at the places where the bishop rested and taught. It was an itinerant band of church artists and workmen, accompanying an itinerant missionary bishop, and doing work that should permanently mark the places where he executed his mission. What was that work? Wilfrith's journeymen

Bede tells us* that until Oswald erected his high wooden cross at Hefenfelth or Hefenfeld, the Heavenly Field on which he defeated the pagans and won his kingdom, there was no *signum* of the Christian faith, no church, no altar, erected in all the land of the Bernicians. The stone

* *H.E.* iii. 2.

minster at York was in Deira, the southern part of Northumbria. The *signum* was the cross; what was the altar, mentioned as something separate from a church? Bede's remark makes it quite clear that he is contrasting the state of things in 636 with the abundance of crosses and altars existing in his own time. This in itself has force for our claim of earliness.

Crosses and Altars

We learn from his famous letter to Ecgbert, the Bishop of York, who on Bede's advice became Archbishop, that the work of maintaining Christianity was still in his time in the hands of itinerant priests, the bishop going about to perform the rite of Confirmation. The itinerant priests attended to the ministration of Baptism and Holy Communion. This tells us what Wilfrith's artists did. They carved and erected a stone cross, to mark the place to which the visiting priest would come at intervals, and there are some reasons for believing that Wilfrith took possession of the spot in the name of some Saint whose day was nearest, or near, to the day on which the cross was erected. But they also carved and erected another stone, not so high as the cross, quite a short shaft with a flat top, and this was the altar. The priest or the bishop brought with him a "portable altar," a small thin slab of valuable stone, or of silver, or of wood ornamented, and on this, laid on the stone altar, the elements were consecrated. Round about these two sculptured stones, those who died in the faith were buried.

The Pontifical of this same Ecgbert, who was the head-master of my own school of York, the only place so far as we know that Bede left his monastery to visit, helps us much in this realisation. In consecrating a church, he consecrated separately the altar. When that was done, he consecrated separately, and as the culminating rite, the *tabula altaris*, the table of the altar, on which the consecrated elements were to rest. This *tabula* was let into the altar, with a cavity for relics beneath it; but for itinerant purposes a portable tabula was used. We have St Cuthbert's tabula, of oak covered with embossed silver*, described on page 34.

Cemeteries and Churches

Further light is thrown upon this matter by the form for consecration of a cemetery in Ecgbert's Pontifical†. At the four corners of the enclosure prayers were said; then at the centre of the enclosure further prayers were said, and the Holy Mysteries were celebrated. Here no doubt was the fixed stone altar and the stone cross, erected in the earliest stages of Christianity. When they eventually built a church, they would naturally not disturb the faithful dead, nor place the church where it would keep the blessed sun from resting on their graves. It would go to the centre

---

* Figured in *Theodore and Wilfrith*, page 105.
† Ecgbert was born about 700, and died in 766.

of the north side of the enclosure. Hence the feeling against burying on the north side of the church, which was outside the consecrated area, and also the feeling against having windows on the north side through which the evil spirits might pry upon the mysteries*. Hence also the central position of the churchyard cross, where the site is very ancient and retains its original dimensions. When a church stands in the middle of a churchyard, the presumption is that it was built when first a site was given to serve as a churchyard.

These considerations provide plenty of work for the band of workmen that accompanied Wilfrith, and they aptly explain obscure phenomena.

In this special connection we may note an example of Professor Cook's methods, taken from pages 252 and 253.

"As the memorial high crosses of Ireland do not antedate the 12th century†, as the Danish memorial stones are of the 9th century and later, and as those of the Isle of Man probably lie between 1050 and 1100, or later, it is antecedently improbable that there should be such a memorial cross in the England of the 7th century."

This, as other parts of Professor Cook's painstaking book, shews inability to grasp the facts of the history of the English Church in the 7th century, as compared with anything that is known, or guessed, about Ireland, Denmark, and Man. Those regions have not one example of great stone churches built in the 7th or any other early century, churches so noble that one of them claimed to be the finest church north of the Alps. They have no example of skilled masons brought from the centres of ecclesiastical art to carve stones for religious purposes with patterns brought with them from Lombardy and elsewhere. They have no example of a bishop moving about over large areas of country with workmen to erect at the various halting places stones with religious sculptures to mark the spot where the itinerant priest should take his stand when he came round to perform the several offices of religion. They have no example of a great Christian victory over paganism, the victory that settled for ever the Christian faith in Northumbria, heralded and—as the people of the time unquestionably believed—secured by the erection of a high cross in the year 642 by the king who completed a minster of stone at York a generation before Biscop and Wilfrith. Our records of the earliest Christianity in the north of England shew that it is antecedently probable—not

Antecedent improbability appears in the margin beside paragraph.

---

* See also Biscop's arrangement of his pictures, p. 21.

† Professor Cook takes as gospel Rivoira's imperious utterances in this respect, with which I am not at all satisfied. Fortunately his assertions in regard to Irish crosses do not touch Bewcastle or Ruthwell.

"antecedently improbable"—"that there should be such a memorial cross in the England of the 7th century."

Professor Cook's argument of antecedent improbability is equally against the next century, when the famous crosses of Acca (d. 740) and Ethelwold (d. 740) were sculptured. He would have been on much surer ground if he had argued that from the history of the time and from the fact that without any fresh influx of artists in stone such beautiful crosses were sculptured and erected, it is antecedently certain, not merely probable, that such memorial crosses were put up before the end of the previous century. He might then have proceeded to point out that the whole argument from antecedent considerations was rendered futile by the simple fact that in 1130, his own accepted time for the erection of our two crosses, William of Malmesbury was describing his own examination of precisely such memorial shafts which already in his time were very ancient. They were, indeed, so ancient that he could not understand or interpret them; while others, comparatively so little ancient then as to be perfectly intelligible and legible, were in memory of a king and of a bishop of the later 7th century. The antecedent improbability is closely akin to an antecedent certainty.

Triple Crosses

I have frequently come upon three crosses at the same place, or the remains of three crosses, of early date, as for instance at Burnsall on the upper waters of the Wharfe, where the Church is dedicated to St Wilfrith. It seems clear to me that there was an early practice in Northumbria of setting up three crosses side by side, the one in the middle taller than the others. The well known Ilkley crosses are a good example, as are the less well known but very remarkable crosses at Checkley, half-way between Stafford and Ilam, at which latter place also there have been three. It may be suggested that the intention was to represent the Trinity. It is an interesting fact that the very earliest reference we find in mediaeval times to the existence of ancient crosses in Northumbria points to the presence of more than one cross, and associates the crosses with the name of the first Christian Missionary in Deira. An ancient title deed of the date of Edward II, relating to lands at Easingwold near York, describes the boundaries as running *usque ad cruces Paulini**. The reference suggests that Deira was earlier than Bernicia, Yorkshire than Northumberland, in the erection of sculptured crosses, and that Paulinus himself set the local example which Wilfrith a generation later followed. This is in accordance with Bede's remark in connection with Oswald's erection of a cross at Heavenfeld, that up to that time no cross and no altar had been set up in Bernicia, the distinction being clearly drawn between the southern and

* See my *Augustine and his Companions*, page 183.

the northern parts of Northumbria. There are reasons for believing that Paulinus did in fact penetrate into Bernicia, but his real sphere of work was Edwin's Deiran court and kingdom. It would lead us into too wide a field to enter upon the question of Paulinus's presence and work at Dewsbury, and elsewhere in that Romano-British direction; but it may be well to say that the cross at Whalley which is in its decoration the most like work of the Roman period and the least like the early Anglo-Saxon work is called by tradition the Cross of Paulinus.

One of the ablest of the favourers of an early date is disturbed by the fact that the form of the cross-head at Ruthwell, as indicated by the top key and the bottom key which have been preserved, is practically the same as that of the cross-heads of the 11th century discovered some years ago in the foundations of the Norman Chapter House at Durham. The sameness is in great measure due to arms inserted in the 19th century. From a very long and wide study of Northumbrian remains, some of them early, all pre-Norman, the form of the heads was to me no surprise*. But when you come to study such immense arms of a cross-head as you find at Lastingham and Winwick, you feel astonishment that the sculptors should have risked so great a weight without support. It would have been so helpful to introduce the strengthening principle of a wheel cross. When you examine the shorter cross at Monasterboice, with its exceedingly heavy arms, you feel that the sculptor was driven to employ the beautiful means of support which give us the "wheel" crosses. A glance at the Durham cross-heads suffices to shew that the sculptors desired to use the arms and the centre for a continuous scene, for which the shaft of the cross was not nearly broad enough. I suggest that the Durham cross-heads are examples of fidelity to type in form, accompanied by extreme decadence in the delineation and carving of the human scenes portrayed. On the other hand, the drawing and the carving of the great bird at the head of the cross shewn on Plate VII, 16 are very creditable to the artists. This bird, in this position, is a remarkable link with Ruthwell. Which if either is the prototype, let the decadence of Durham tell.

It is necessary to remark in this connection that David of Scotland was directly under the influence of Durham. Turgot, the Lincolnshire Saxon, became a monk at Jarrow in 1074. In 1083 the Norman Bishop of Durham transferred the monks of Jarrow and Wearmouth to Durham and made them the Chapter of his Cathedral Church. In 1087 Turgot became Prior of Durham. When Margaret of Scotland died, 1093, she

Durham cross-heads

Influence on David

* The Durham cross-heads are not large. The one shewn in Plate VII, 16, is only 2 ft. 9¼ in. across the arms.

entrusted her children to Turgot's care, her husband Malcolm III being still alive. In 1107 Alexander succeeded to the throne of Scotland, and being determined to put an end to the Culdee succession in his land, he had Turgot consecrated to St Andrews. Turgot died there in 1115, when his pupil young David had been Prince of Cumbria for eight years.

The Durham cross-heads were smashed by the Normans when they began to build the new Cathedral Church. The foundation stones of that building were laid by Bishop William and Prior Turgot on August 11, 1093, three months before Margaret left David and his brothers in Turgot's charge. He would be a hardy historian who suggested the despised and smashed cross-heads as the honoured type from which the cross-head at Ruthwell was copied by the Prince of Cumbria under Turgot's stauroclastic influence. It is remarkable that at Durham as at Jedburgh* we find this telling evidence of the vandalism of Professor Cook's artistic heroes.

St Andrews Turgot founded at St Andrews the new church establishment and the new church. Here if anywhere we ought to find the evidences that David's leader in art work could produce decoration comparable with Ruthwell. The sculptured remains of the previous establishment at Kilrimont are well known; they are of course of a class fundamentally different from the work at Ruthwell; they are of the Pictish type. The remains of the work of the post-conquest churchmen at St Andrews Rivoira himself has carefully examined†. Anything poorer, or less like the beauty of the work at Ruthwell, it would be difficult to find. The St Andrews work is a strong argument against Professor Cook's Davidian origin. It seems to me to be fatal to Rivoira, who has fully acquainted himself with the work at St Andrews.

Along with the cross-heads at Durham some quite first-rate interlacements were found on a fine grave-cover, shewing that the monks had kept up that branch of art at a high point of excellence, both in design and in sculpture, as we might be quite sure they would.

This present age has seen the erection of two noble crosses in memory of Bede the Historian and Caedmon the Poet. On the vigorous initiative of Canon Rawnsley, a number of us determined in 1898 that these two great men must no longer remain without a witness in their own Northumbria. We secured the help of Mr C. C. Hodges of Hexham, whose unrivalled knowledge and facility of design enabled him to produce monuments not inferior to the design of the Bewcastle and Ruthwell Crosses. Caedmon's Cross, which we erected in the churchyard at his own Whitby, is 19 ft. 6 in. high, about 2 ft. higher than the Ruthwell Cross. The flowing vine,

* See pages 7, 8.   † *Burlington Magazine*, XXI. 15.

which covers two of the sides at Ruthwell, is replaced by the wild rose on one face and the English apple on the other. The figures we selected are, Our Lord in blessing, David playing the harp, the Abbess Hild, Caedmon himself, and four of the Whitby students of his period (A.D. 680), Bosa, Aetla, Oftfor, and John, all of whom, as well as their famous fellow-student Wilfrith, became bishops. We incised on the face, in modern English, and also in Anglo-Saxon both in runes and in minuscules, the nine lines of Caedmon's first sacred song on the Creation, beginning

> Now must we praise
> The Warder of Heaven's realm
> The Creator's might
> And His mind's thought
> The works of the glorious Father.

The Poet Laureate, Alfred Austin, inaugurated the Cross for us.

The Bede Cross is higher still, I think too high, 25 feet. It stands in clear air at Roker Point, the fumes of chemical works at Jarrow rendering it unwise to erect it nearer Bede's home. The inscriptions are in Bede's own words, first his death-song, in Anglo-Saxon in runes and in modern English block letters, and then passages from his writings. I selected these from his prefaces to the *Ecclesiastical History of the English* and the *Life of St Cuthbert*, as an example of minute care for all writers of history. These are in the bold script of Acca's Cross. There are busts of several of Bede's contemporaries, the kings Ecgfrith and Ceolwulf, Bishops Acca and Ecgbercht (afterwards Archbishop), Abbats Benedict Biscop, Eosterwine, Siegfrith, Ceolfrith of the Codex Amiatinus, and Huaetbercht, Trumbercht Doctor, and John Arch Chanter. There are five bas-reliefs of scenes from Bede's life. The Cross was unveiled on October 11, 1904, by the Archbishop of York, the Bishop of Durham taking part in the ceremony. The surface ornament is beautiful. It comes nearer to a representation of one of the marvellous pages of the Lindisfarne Gospels than anything else that can be shewn.

CHAPTER V

The ivory chair.—Its history.—Solomon's ivory throne.—Otto III.—Salona and Spalato.—
Monograms.—Maximianus.—The subjects of the *tavolette*.—Vine scrolls in Rome.—Eastern
provenance of the ivory chair.—Biscop and Wilfrith.—The Church of Aurona, Milan.—
S. Salvatore, Brescia.—Arian Baptisteries and Crosses.—Controversy on the symbolism of
the Lamb.—The Quinisext Council.—Crosses at Bologna and Beverley.—Pre-historic
imports from Italy.

I must now turn to our most important positive evidence of the use
of vine scrolls with birds and animals, in combination with an abundance
of scenes from the New Testament, more than a century before the earliest
date we propose for our crosses. The evidence is found on the great ivory
chair of Maximianus (Plates I, II, III), the Archbishop of Ravenna (546–
556) who consecrated the church of S. Vitale there, and whose name
appears on the great mosaic of Justinian and his court in that church.

The first mention we have of this chair is in the year 1001, when the
doge of Venice, Pietro Orseolo II, into whose hands it had fallen, presented
it to the emperor Otto III, who gave it to Ravenna. It is described by
John the Deacon, who conveyed it to the emperor, as a *cathedra* artistically
carved with panels of ivory.

I see that on March 6, 1888, I said here in Cambridge, speaking of
Maximian's Chair, "This beautiful work of art, which some of us had the
opportunity of examining long and closely last Easter, quite puts an end
to all question of the possibility of the sculptured works of Anglian Art
being produced in the 7th century. Nothing was wanted but the design
and the sculptor. There was a School of Christian Art ready to produce
both, and we are distinctly told that our Anglian forefathers brought with
them on their return from Italy both the art and the artists." Since
that time I have more than once mentioned the chair as a probable
source of inspiration for the artists of our two great monuments. Professor
Cook quotes (p. 285) from one of my books, "G. F. Browne, Bishop of Bristol,
has expressed the feeling that on the upright on either side of the chair
you have the secret of the original of this most beautiful side of the Bewcastle Cross"—that is, the side with the continuous vine scroll—and adds,
"Unfortunately for this theory, it has been shown that the throne was not
sent to Ravenna till the year 1001." I have tried, without success, to
follow the workings of the writer's mind in this last remark. In the first

place, no such thing has been shewn; all that has been shewn is that it The Ravenna Chair was sent to Ravenna in 1001. As the story unfolds itself, we shall see curiously clear reason for holding that Ravenna was its original home at the period 546–556. But that flaw in the statement, though vitally important as a matter of accuracy on an actively controversial point, is a mere nothing to the misfit of the argument as affecting the chair as a source of inspiration. What does it matter where the chair was when the 7th century artists studied it? Unless Professor Cook is able to shew reason why the chair must be dated later than our period, the latter half of the 7th century, his argument appears to be quite useless. He does not make any such suggestion, and if he did he would have the Italians and so far as I know every one who knows against him. Professor Cook had presumably not seen the chair or known what the subjects of the carved ivory tablets were; otherwise he could not have written as he has of the Baptist with the Lamb, the Annunciation and the Visitation, or the Flight into Egypt. Ricci, from whose translation in Italian from the original Latin of John the Deacon* he quotes, adds that the work is Eastern, from Byzantium or Alexandria or Antioch. Carotti, from whom he quotes, states that it is "an Alexandrian work of the sixth century," and adds that it was first taken from Alexandria to Grado, and then in 1001 to Ravenna. But that story of its earliest *provenance* was found to be due to a confusion with the chair of St Mark, and is abandoned.

It was certain that in Eastern lands the example of Solomon would Solomon's throne be followed, as no doubt Solomon followed the example of the kings of more ancient countries. He "made a great throne of ivory and overlaid it with the best gold." The Septuagint Version has "he encircled it with gold of proof"; the Vulgate, "he clothed it with gold." The back of Solomon's chair was round, as Maximian's. There were "stays (margin *hands*) on either side on the place of the seat." The Vulgate has 'hands,' as also the Greek. The Revised Version gives 'arms' as the alternative to 'stays,' and states that the Hebrew word means 'hands.' The Septuagint Version is of course that which the oriental Greek artist used, and it has a very curious variation from the phrase "the top of the throne was round behind." The Greek rendering is, "the throne had the countenances of calves from the hinder part thereof." The whole account has kinship with Maximian's chair, the belts of beaten gold and the countenances of calves being represented by the ivory framework of the tavolette. The record of Solomon's imports of ivory and peacocks evidently had a direct bearing upon the art of the Church of the East, which judiciously disregarded the companion import, apes.

* Pertz, *Hist. Germ. Mon.* I. 34.

Otto III Otto did not get this chair for nothing. We have an interesting story of his attitude towards presents. He was three times at Ravenna in 1001. His documents shew* that he was there March 25 to May 12, also September 11 to 21, and November 20 to December 12. Early in the year he had paid a visit to the doge in very strict disguise. On this occasion the doge pressed gifts upon him. But the emperor refused them, declaring that he would not run the risk of being charged with having come to receive presents and not for love of San Marco and the doge. He did unwillingly accept an ivory *sedile* with its *subsellium*, and a silver siphon and ewer rarely wrought. In November he sent to the doge, by John, two imperial ornaments wonderfully wrought in gold, one from Pavia and one from Ravenna. The doge in return sent to him a *cathedra* skilfully carved with panels of ivory. This, as we have seen, the emperor received with avidity, and he left it to be preserved in the city.

In the Italian Art Magazine, *Felix Ravenna*, for July 1912, Giambattista Cervellini writes (pages 278–291) on the arrangement of the tavolette on the ivory chair of Ravenna. The article is full of information and interest†.

Salona Cervellini reports that a paper was read to the National Society of Antiquaries of France on 8 June 1910 by M. Martroye, maintaining that this could not be the chair of Maximianus of Ravenna, because it could not be explained how it came into the possession of the doge. The monogram, he said, could be read "Maximus Episcopus." We may fairly disagree with that reading, as inadequate‡. There was, he says, a bishop Maximus§ at Salona in 342. The Goths and Avars ruined Salona. The remains of Maximus were preserved in a church built in his honour in the middle of the city, from which the doge of Venice carried it off, after encountering a dogged resistance, when he took Salona. On his return from the war (997) he assumed the title of duke, and gave to Otho the episcopal chair which he had brought with him thence. There was a later bishop Maximus‖ at Salona, 593–620, but Martroye rejects him, because he was archbishop, and the monogram reads bishop.

Spalato This account of a fight for a chair in the centre of the city of Salona in 997 is not in accordance with what we know of that famous place. The great Roman city Salona was destroyed by the Avars in 639. Three miles distant was Spalato, where Diocletian had built his villa, and where he lived for some eight years and died. At this spot the fugitives from

* I owe much of my information about this emperor to the Keeper of the Archives at Oxford, Dr R. L. Poole. The monograms of Otto and his father Otto II are clumsy as compared with the two skilful monograms of Maximianus of Ravenna.

† Professor Baldwin Brown called attention to it in the *Burlington Magazine*, XXIII. 44.

‡ It is evident in both monograms that *N* is one of the letters of the name.

§ Maximus III.   ‖ Maximus IV.

Salona settled, after their first hurried flight to a number of the neighbouring islands. An attempt was made by them to restore Salona but was soon abandoned, and in 650 Spalato became the archiepiscopal city, the title of Salona being retained into the Middle Ages. The people of Spalato sent an expedition to Salona to recover the remains of their popular Saint Domnius. His basilica was found to be in ruins and overgrown with brambles, but they found his coffin and it was translated to Spalato with great pomp, to a new resting place in the Cathedral Church which the people had built. There was, 300 years later, a great Venetian expedition at the time to which M. Martroye refers, under the doge Pietro Orseolo II, and Spalato took the oath of allegiance to Venice.

Cervellini remarks that the chair cannot be of the fourth century date, because the ornamentation is not, in the opinion of the best students, earlier than the sixth century. He adds, however, that the difference of opinion may be explained by the suggestion that the front of the chair, where the Saints are, has elements of the fourth century, and is of earlier date than the tablets of ivory with Scripture subjects.

The monogram on the chair has been the subject of much discussion The monogram in Italy. The first modern attempt to decipher it was made in 1690 by Mario Fiorentini; his letter, written from Lucca, is in the archiepiscopal archives at Ravenna. He read it Maximianus Episcopus, and attributed it to the great archbishop of that name, 546–556.

Last autumn a very remarkable confirmation of this attribution appeared*. A quantity of marble rubbish was being removed from the Archiepiscopal Palace, when the workmen came upon a *pulvino* of Greek marble, one side of which was unbroken. On that side was found a monogram identical with this on the chair, except that a Latin cross took the place of the S, and the S was formed by using the semi-circular top of the P as the lower half of an S. This really remarkable discovery completely establishes the chair in its rightful original home. See figure *d*.

d. Monogram of Maximianos.

The *Liber Pontificalis* of Agnellus† tells us that Maximian ordered a most precious altar-cloth of byssus, on which was embroidered the whole history of the Saviour. "It is not possible to imagine the human figures or the beasts and birds which are made on it." This directly denies the asserted lateness of such scenes as those at Ruthwell, and strongly supports the attribution of the chair to Maximian, 546–556.

* Gerola, *Felix Ravenna*, fasc. 19, 1915.
† *S. Sophia* (*Constantinople*), Lethaby and Swainson, p. 71.

It has been objected that the ivory chair had not any history known to Otto III which should induce him to hand over to Ravenna so splendid a gift. I can have no doubt that the monogram was history enough for him. The objectors appear to forget the immense importance attached by rulers of Italy and Germany to their monograms. Anyone who has seen their diplomas knows this. Otto must very often have seen the remarkable monograms of his Carolingian predecessors. He was himself very careful about his own authenticating monogram. He had three in his time. The first was only the letters of his name. The next had a letter noting his kingly rank inwoven. The one he used as emperor had imperial letters inwoven. So great was his personal attention to this matter of highest importance, the validation of his documents, that in the six years during which he was emperor, he had no less than seven different types of seal. And it is evident from the chronicles that he was keenly alive to external impressions.

When, in Ravenna, Otto read this monogram as *Maximianos Episcopos*, and looked up at the great mosaic of his predecessor Justinian who reigned there, and saw *Maximianus* in large capitals, the only name given in the whole court of Justinian and Theodora, he must have felt sure that he was restoring to Ravenna the chair in which the archbishop was wont to sit on the occasion of great ceremonies, such as the consecration of S. Vitale. It was as authentic as one of his own precepts stamped with his own authoritative monogram. "He received it with avidity" and left it in its old home.

As to how it came to leave its home we need not stop to enquire. The emperor knew too much of the ways of emperors and people of that kind to have any difficulty. Charlemagne himself had carried off from Ravenna the bronze statue of Theodoric, and had taken the columns of his palace to Aachen; probably the chair had before his time been carried off at some change of dynasty, as when the Lombards came or when the Lombards left. The Venetians, too, were an acquisitive and commercial people, and Ravenna was handy for them. They may well have become possessed of the chair in the course of business or mercenary warfare. A valuable property like this might serve to lubricate a transaction.

I may in passing say that there is no force in Martroye's argument that this cannot have been an archbishop's chair, because the original proprietor is described in the monogram as bishop. A very slight acquaintance with inscriptions is sufficient to explode the argument. In the duomo of Ravenna itself we have the great ambo of Maximianus's successor in the archbishopric, Agnellus, with the inscription AGNELLUS EPISC HUNC PYRGUM &c. And it may be suggested that after all the *archi* is in fact present in the monogram. All you have to do is to take X and P as both Greek and Latin capitals, and you have Archiepiscopos*.

The mention of the ambo or pyrgus of Agnellus may remind us of a suggestive similarity between the work of the two archbishops. Each is covered with rectangular tablets, with arabesque frames, and the curved part of the pyrgus has twenty-four of these tablets, as have the curved parts of the ivory chair.

Cervellini informs us that of the numerous missing tavolette several have been restored to Ravenna since 1887, when I was there and procured the photographs from which Mr Emery Walker has produced the photogravures shewn on Plates I, II, III. I shewed slides of the chair, made from these photographs, at Cambridge in 1890, and in a lecture at the South Kensington Museum about the same time; as also at Bristol, some ten years later. I had dealt with it in a Disney lecture in 1888. *[margin: Subjects of the tavolette]*

In 1893 the existence of four portions of the missing pieces was known. At Naples there was the Jesus and the Samaritan woman; at Pesaro the Annunciation and the Multiplication of the Loaves; at Rome, in the Stroganoff collection, the Manger and the Entry into Jerusalem; at Milan, the Healing of the Blind. Between 1893 and 1905 all of these were restored to Ravenna. Of the eight tablets on the front of the chair and the sixteen on the back, sixteen in all are now accounted for.

Cervellini arranges the tablets in pairs. In the time of Muratori the scenes were

    A. f. The Magi (two scenes)
       b. The Baptism
    B. f. The Trial by Water†
       b. The Multiplication of the Loaves
    C. f. The Visitation
       b. The Feast at Cana

this last was afterwards lost.

* The monogram of Euphrasius, who was building the duomo of Parenzo while S. Vitale was being built in Ravenna, and building it with a delicacy of carving and undercutting which to say the least rivals that of S. Vitale, appears in many parts of the duomo. It is a very poor monogram as compared with that on the ivory chair. When his name appears in an inscription the word Episcopus is given as Eps. and it appears so in the monogram. Thus the letter *o* is not required, the letter *s* being inserted alone in the field, as on the ivory chair.

† *Prova del Acqua.* This is a scene from the Apocryphal Gospels, the judicial trial of the Virgin Mary by the Test of Water. In the Book of Numbers, ch. v, verses 11–31, the "law of jealousies" is laid down, as between man and woman. The Pseudo-Matthew Gospel, ch. xii, describes its application to the Virgin and to Joseph. First Joseph was summoned to the altar and made to drink of the holy water, in which dust had been put from the floor of the tabernacle. He then walked seven times round the altar, and no change appeared on his countenance, as would have been the case if he had done wrong. The same was done in the case of Mary, and her countenance, too, underwent no change. So both were declared clean.

Removed from its place, but still preserved in the Duomo, is

D. f. The going to Bethlehem

   b. The Marriage at Cana (two scenes)

Restored later

E.   Jesus and the Samaritan Woman

F. f. The Annunciation

   b. The Multiplication of the Loaves

G. f. The Manger

   b. The Entry into Jerusalem

H.   The Healing of the Blind (still loose, not fixed)

This accounts for sixteen, of which seven were in front, where there are eight spaces.

Another tavoletta, which cannot be found, is known to have had

I. f. The Adoration of the Magi

   b. The Flight into Egypt

but it is not certain that this belonged to the chair.

The sides of the chair are covered with scenes from the history of Joseph, with large numbers of human figures. The subjects stand out very clearly, and are graphically treated. In front are five very good figures, St John Baptist in the centre, and the Evangelists two on each side. These figures are distinctly very early in type. On the selection of the Baptist as the companion figure to Our Lord at Bewcastle and Ruthwell, see page 28.

The decoration The decoration of the upright posts in front of the chair might have been taken as the ground of the two great vine scrolls at Ruthwell and the one at Bewcastle; except that the spaces on the posts of the chair are not broad enough to allow the active life of the birds and beasts to be shewn. The decoration of the frames and bands throughout is of this same character; vine scrolls, birds, and animals; and it is much more living where the spaces are more adequate.

Vine scrolls in Rome Of course there are plenty of examples in Rome of these scrolls and birds, nowhere, as far as I remember, so free as at Bewcastle and Ruthwell. You have them in the catacomb of Prætextatus, on posts in the Forum, in the cloister wall of S. Lorenzo Fuori, in the porch of Sti Apostoli, indeed pretty well all over if you have your eyes open for them. The roof of the circular aisle of Sta Costanza has a lovely wilderness of scrolls of the vine, with birds and bunches of grapes and little genii variously occupied. The wonder would be if we had not examples of like kind in England, dating from the time when Biscop and Wilfrith, men much in advance of their time here, made journey after journey to places where they saw these things, and fell passionately in love with what they saw.

There is abundant reason for assigning the origin—quite probably Eastern origin the manufacture—of this chair to Egypt, certainly to directly Eastern influence. The work of English scholars of recent years has left no doubt at all on this point. Under the general name "Byzantine," which notes a centre of distribution rather than of production, we now understand that wide areas of Asia and Africa are covered by the term. Indeed the evidence which points to Coptic art as the origin of much that we find in Europe and of some things which we find in these islands is becoming strong.

In my judgment, this ivory chair is in itself sufficient to sweep away Evidence of the chair Professor Cook's questionings as to whether such scenes as we find on the Ruthwell Cross could be as early as we claim, and also his resort to 12th century work at Chartres for the origin of the lovely vine scrolls at Ruthwell and Bewcastle. And there can be no doubt that other examples of like kind were before the eyes of Biscop and of Wilfrith as they journeyed through Italy bent upon seeing the best church art of that rich and spacious period of Eastern Art in Italy. Nor can there be any doubt that the skilled stone-cutters and architects whom they brought over to England, to carry out like work here, had their portfolios full of the choicest patterns of panels in wood and stone and ivory. Nor, again, any doubt that when artists did not specialise as they do now, but covered the whole area of decorative art, those same folios had abundance of examples of the writing and the decoration of noble manuscripts and their jewelled covers. It was not the only book of the kind, that won the heart of the youthful Wilfrith on his first visit to Rome, and led to the production, here on English soil, of a Gospel-book of like pre-eminence of richness and of beauty.

I may quote here a passage from the appendix to my *Conversion of the Heptarchy*. It was added after the book was completed, as the result of another exploration in Milan for illustrations of my theory.

There are two shafts, each more than seven feet high and about a foot Milan square at bottom and ten inches at top, in the Archaeological Museum (at the Brera) in Milan, which it is impossible to disregard in connection with the question of the originals of our great Anglian cross-shafts. They are from the long-ruined church called the Church of Aurona, opened up not long ago in the course of excavations in the streets of Milan. On two capitals found among the ruins there is an inscription in Latin, *Here rests the Lord Archbishop Theodore who was unjustly condemned. Julian made me thus beautiful**.

---

* "Julianus me fecit sic pulchrum." I am inclined to suspect a play upon the words "sic pulchrum" and "sepulchrum."

These must have been the capitals of columns supporting the sarcophagus of Archbishop Theodore of Milan, who was murdered in 739. The church was named after Theodore's sister, Aurona; it may have been built to hold the sarcophagus, but it appears to have been of an earlier date than that.

Art in Lombardy

The two shafts probably reveal to us the state of Christian art in Lombardy in the period to which we assign the inspiration of the crosses forming the subject of this essay. One of the shafts has a socket hole cut out at the top, and this may have served to hold a cross; or they may have been the supports of an architrave. They have on all four sides flowing scrolls, some double, forming ovals as on the south side of the Bewcastle Cross and on Acca's Cross, with tendrils passing off alternately left and right. The ovals contain leaf-ornaments, the tendrils end in vine-leaves, grapes, etc. They have not birds and animals in them; but in one case there is a single bird at the top, and in the other case a single quadruped. These creatures are very rudely executed, as rudely as the quadruped on the Bakewell Cross; but all the rest of the work is beautiful. There is at Brescia a similar shaft, with poor interlacements on all of its faces. It is 8th century work, from the church of S. Salvatore, whence comes also the noble peacock sculpture of the same period, with its grape and leaf arabesques and its long border of good interlacement. Cattaneo (Venezia, 1888) figures these on pages 126, 127, of his book *L'Architettura in Italia dal secolo vi al mille circa*. Commendatore Rivoira tells us (English edition, i. 136) that San Salvatore was begun in 753 and built by King Desiderius (756–774). Some of its features come from the earlier church of St Michael and St Peter on the same site, the 6th century work of Greek carvers.

Symbolism of the Lamb

The question of the presence in England of a number of realistic subjects from the New Testament towards the end of the 7th century, is one of deeper significance than any mere question of art, however interesting and important such questions may be. It touches the reality of the Life and Sufferings of Our Lord and Saviour.

You see in the great Arian Baptistry at Ravenna the magnificent circle of the apostles, and in the place where the Lord should be, a throne set, with robes laid on it. On the white marble Arian crosses, which gleam so bright in their red-brick setting, you see only a graceful decoration of flowers. On the sarcophagus of Junius Bassus—I am not keeping any order, chronological or otherwise—you have the miracles of the Lord and of the Old Testament performed by lambs. A lamb strikes the rock for water, a lamb changes the water into wine, a lamb baptises a smaller lamb, a lamb touches a mummy Lazarus with a wand, and a lamb receives the tables of the law. The lamb appears in the mosaics of the chapel of Galla Placidia, and a lamb is prominent on the capitals of S. Vitale. The lamb appeared on the Cross in place of Our Lord, and appeared on altars in pictorial representations as the Sacrifice. I shew on Plate VI, 10, an example in our own land, on the remarkable grave-cover at Wirksworth in Derbyshire. There was a general tendency to keep in the background the reality of the human life of Our Lord, the reality of His suffering.

Against this tendency one school of art had specially striven. I am inclined to think that this school was Greek, or was mainly favoured by the Greeks, though it is a balanced question. I regard the ivory chair of Ravenna as a masterpiece of this orthodox school. It looks to the East, not to the West, to Constantinople, not to Rome. A chair, however archiepiscopal, was not a fitting place for some of the scenes of Our Lord's life, or for a great representation of the Lord, but the realities and the details of that Life are there in abundance. _{An ortho-dox school}

Now our subject takes us into the later part of the seventh century. In that century the struggle between these two schools came to a head. It had long been going on. Biscop must have heard much of it from Theodore; Hadrian from Egypt; Wilfrith from the southern slopes of the Alps, where at Brescia there is still a noble ivory casket, not unlike the Werden casket whose plaques are in the South Kensington Museum, with beautifully carved scenes from the New Testament. I take it that under those influences England was on the right side. Some fifteen years before Wilfrith passed away, probably within a twelve-month of the death of Biscop, a great Council was held at Constantinople, when it was ordered that the Saviour should be represented in His human form, not under the figure of a lamb. That settled the principle. The reason assigned was, that the people might have their thoughts turned to His Passion and saving Death, and through His humiliation might learn His glory. That was the language used at Constantinople in 691. One feels a little impatient when writers call in question the possibility of a particular scene from the New Testament appearing on an English cross about the very time when this council ended a long controversy*.

I find that on March 6, 1888, after dwelling at some length upon the ivory chair, I proceeded to link Ravenna with Bologna, and Bologna with Northumbria, by means of the Arian and other decorated crosses, free

---

* The date of the Quinisext Council (supplementary to the Fifth and Sixth General Councils) is uncertain. The balance of opinion seems to be in favour of 691. Biscop died in 690.

from any indication of suffering, and ornamented with flowers and scrolls, which still exist at Ravenna.

Bologna There are in the nave of S. Petronio, the church in Bologna which holds the place of a cathedral church, a number of Latin crosses, of comparatively small size, set on the top of pedestals I think some 8 or 10 feet high. I was told that there are three other crosses like these in other churches at Bologna. They have the air of great though possibly not very great antiquity.. They are the only things that I know anywhere which are in any very marked way like the numerous remains of crosses which we possess. The resemblance is striking if merely accidental. The priests in charge very kindly had ladders brought for me, and helped to take rubbings, some of which I reproduced by photolithography for my class in Cambridge.

These crosses were for very long placed at the entrances to Bologna, and there are inscriptions to this effect on the pedestals, with the dedication of each cross. One, by far the rudest of them all, but the nearest perhaps except in rudeness to Anglian design, is the cross of the Holy Virgins, originally erected on the Via Castilionia. Another was the cross of the Apostles and Evangelists, originally erected at the Ravenna gate of Bologna. Another, with a lamb and cross in the centre, is the cross of the Holy Martyrs, originally erected at the Porta Castellana.

We have, among other evidences in England, an interesting account of the erection of beautifully sculptured crosses at the entrance to Beverley in Yorkshire. Athelstan, who reigned from 924 to 940, and had intimate relations with the continent by the marriage of one sister with Hugh the Great, Count of Paris, and of another with Otho*, son of Henry the Fowler made special arrangements for the right of sanctuary at Beverley. There were six degrees of peace or safety; (1) from a certain cross in the country to the crosses which Athelstan set up—*nobiliter insculptae*—at the entrance to Beverley, on either side the way, (2) from these crosses to the church porch, (3) from the porch to the door, (4) from the door to the choir, (5) from the choir to the presbytery, (6) to the frithstol or stone seat of peace, where every fugitive had full protection. The frithstol is in the church still, as is Wilfrith's at Hexham. These nobly sculptured sanctuary crosses, Professor Cook should note, are 200 years before 1125, and only 200 years later than Acca and Ethelwold.

It may be mentioned as a quaint coincidence, though with no bearing upon our present subject, that just when this chapter was being written, with its general references to Italian influence here, and special reference

---

* The grandfather of Otto III who restored the ivory chair to Ravenna.

to Bologna and Venice, a paper was read at the Society of Antiquaries of which a summary was given in the *Athenæum*. "The bronze vessels of the principal phase of the Hallstatt period could be traced to Bologna, and belonged to the Villanova civilisation of the 8th century B.C.; whereas the later buckets, with narrow cordons, were distributed over Europe from the Venetian area, and one had been found as far afield as Weybridge. There were other indications of the importation of Italian objects into Britain during the Hallstatt period, and more would probably come to light."

CHAPTER VI

The Dream of the Holy Rood.—One of Caedmon's poems —The Quinisext Council.—Kedmon
mæ fauœda.—Six readings compared.—The spelling *Kedmon*.—The Cross of Drahmal.—
The word *thun*.—The words *æft*, *æfter*.—King Oswin.—Phonetic spelling.—Professor Cook
and *Gessus Kristtus*.—*Cynnburug*.—Mistakes in inscriptions.—Local pronunciation.—Inscriptions not altered like manuscripts.—Lateness of two runes.—Lul's runic alphabet.—
The Anglian futhork.

THE DREAM OF THE HOLY ROOD

Those parts which can be read on the Ruthwell Cross are printed in italic letters.

List! a dream of dreams is now my theme.
'Twas midnight when the vision met my gaze;
hushed was the speech of men in silent rest.
Methought I there beheld a wondrous tree,
borne aloft, all wrapt about with light;
never was tree so bright; it was a beacon
of molten gold, and gems shone forth therefrom,
four below, nigh earth, and five above
on the spreading arms; God's angels, ever-fair,
gazed on 't,—*a gallows-tree, but not of shame*;
angels and holy spirits gazed thereon,
and men on earth, yea, all *creation*,—
a wondrous tree of triumph! and sin-stained I,
wounded with guilt, I saw that glorious tree
shining so brightly in its golden gear,
its rich adornments; the staff of sovran might
right fittingly was all bedight with gems.
But yet, e'en through the gold might I discern
the pangs they felt, those sufferers of old,
when first the blood o'er its right side streamed
    forth.
I, too, was sore perturbed; the wondrous sight
thrilled me with fear: I saw the hast'ning beacon
changing in garb and hue, now damped with wet,
and soiled with running blood, now decked with
    gold.
Long lay I there, and long I gazed thereat,
and, sad in soul, beheld the Saviour's tree,
until I heard how it gave forth a voice;
and these words spake to me that holiest wood :—
"'Twas long ago, yet I remember well,
how I was hewn adown at the forest's edge,
cut from my stem, and strong foes took me thence;
made me a spectacle; bade me bear their outcasts;
bore me on their shoulders; set me on a hill;

foes fixed me there. Then saw I mankind's Lord
hastening in His might to ascend me there:
I dared not then oppose the word of God,
or bend or break asunder, though I saw
earth's bosom quake; yea, all His foes might I
have laid full low, yet stood I firm.
Then the young warrior prepared himself—
'twas God Almighty, resolute and strong;
brave, in the sight of many, He went up
upon the lofty cross, to save mankind.
I trembled in His clasp, yet dared not bow,
or fall to earth; I had to stand there firm.
A cross they stood me there; I uplifted the great King,
the Lord of Heaven, and yet I dared not stoop.
They pierced me with dark nails: you see the wounds,
the open gashes; I durst harm none of them.
They scorned us both together. Stained was I
with the blood that streamed forth from His side,
    when He,
as man, had sent His spirit on its way.
Many a bitter pang endured I there,
upon that mount; I saw the Lord of Hosts
cruelly bestead; I saw the darkness shroud
with covering of clouds the Ruler's corse;
day's splendour fled before the shades of night,
wan 'neath the welkin. All creation wept;
their King's fall mourned they; *Christ was on the*
    Cross.
Then men came thither, hastening from afar
unto their noble Prince. All this saw I.
Sore pained, I bowed me to the hands of men,
humbly, with all my strength. Then took they
    thence
Almighty God, and raised Him from the rack;
but me the warriors left, standing forlorn,

bespattered all with blood, *wounded with shafts.*
Him they laid down, limb-weary; stood by His head;
they looked upon the Lord of Heaven; and there
    awhile
He rested, harassed by that mighty toil.
Then 'gan they make an earthy grave for Him,
in the sight of His foes; they wrought it of bright
    stone;
and laid therein the Lord of Victory;
then over Him they sang a mournful dirge,
sadly, at eventide, when they must leave,
with heavy hearts, the Great King resting there,
with no great retinue to guard His rest.
We, crosses, stood there in our place awhile,
weeping, until anon fierce warriors came—
(the body, life's fair dwelling, was then cold)—
and therewithal they felled us to the earth,
and (dreadful fate!) in a deep pit they hid us;
but me the servants of the Lord found there;
with silver and with gold they decked me o'er.
Now mayst thou hear, thou dear beloved friend,
what deeds of baleful men, what direful griefs,
I once endured; but now the time is come,
and, far and wide, all men throughout the earth,
yea, all this great creation, honour me,
and pray unto this sign. On me God's Son
suffered awhile; wherefore I firmly now
tower high 'neath Heaven, and it is mine to heal
each of mankind who stands in awe of me.
Of yore was I the cruellest punishment,
most loathsome unto men, ere I made clear
the way of Life for all who speak the word.
Lo, me the Prince of glory, Heaven's Lord,
hath glorified above all forest-trees,
as He, Almighty God, hath glorified
His mother, Mary, above womankind.
Now bid I thee, thou dear beloved friend,
to tell aright this Vision unto men;
reveal in words, that 'tis the Tree of Glory,
whereon Almighty God endured dire pangs
for mortals' sins, and Adam's old offence.
The death He tasted there; yet in His might
the Lord arose again to help mankind;
He thence ascended into Heaven; He comes
into the world again to visit folk;
at Doomsday will He come, the Lord Himself,
Almighty God, and angel-hosts with Him,
wielding the power of doom; He then will judge
each man, as he erewhile hath merited,

during the fading days of life on earth.
Not any one may then be free from fear,
when the All-wielding Lord shall speak the word,
when He will ask before that multitude,
where is the man who in God's name would taste
of bitter death, as He did, on the Cross.
They then will dread, and little will they know
wherewith to make reply to Christ's request.
Yet none need there know any touch of fear,
who bears within his breast the best of signs:
yea, by the Cross, the soul of every man,
leaving the track of earth, finds Heaven's realm,
if he but yearn to dwell there with the Lord."
With blithesome mood, with all my spirit's might,
I prayed then to the Cross; I was alone;
no men were with me there; my very soul
was eager for departure; I had endured
too many hours of longing. Life's hope is now
that I may seek that Tree of Victory,
and, all alone, and oftenest of men,
may worthily adore it; my will is set thereon;
'tis strong within my heart: for my defence
I look but to the Rood. Few mighty friends
have I on earth; they have departed hence
from the world's joys; they sought the King of
    Glory;
with the High Father live they now in Heaven;
they dwell in glory; and I, too, day by day,
await the hour when this, the Prince's Cross,
once seen by me on earth, shall fetch me forth
from this poor life, and bring me to that place,
where bliss abounds, and all the heavenly joys,
where at the feast the Sovran's folk doth sit,
where bliss is everlasting. May He then
appoint a place, where I may thenceforth dwell
in glory, sharing with the Just their joys!
The Lord befriend me, He that suffered once
on earth upon the Cross for mankind's sins!
He then redeemed us, and gave life to us,
a home in Heaven. Hope was then renewed,
and bliss and joy, to those who burnt before.
The Son came back as Victor from the fight,
with mighty triumph; with Him a multitude,
a troop of souls, the mighty Sovran brought
into God's kingdom. Joy to angels, joy
to all the Saints then dwelling there in glory,
in Heaven's heights, when He, their Ruler, came,
the Lord Almighty, back unto His realm.

I have printed as a preface to discussion the translation of the "Dream of the Holy Rood" which Dr Gollancz made for me twenty years ago for my book on Theodore and Wilfrith. There seem to me to be good reasons for attributing the earlier and finer half of this great poem to Caedmon, down to the words "harassed by that mighty toil." Simplicity of thought and diction ceases at the point indicated.

Bede

Bede, writing about 730, says that others of the English race after Caedmon had made religious poems, but none could equal his poems because they were produced by free gift from above. Thus Caedmon has no competitors for the authorship of this poem in Bede's time. And Bede tells us how Caedmon's poems were first produced. The rulers of the monastery expounded to him a passage of sacred history or doctrine. In his dreams it was formed into a poem, and in the morning he dictated it to a scribe. There could not be many, among his poems, to excel this one in beauty and power.

Now the "Dream of the Rood" is essentially, in the part specified, a dream. It is produced, as only Caedmon's poems were, entirely in a dream. After that, it wanders off into the finding of the three crosses, and much holy meditation, and, as I think, ceases to be Caedmon's.

Quinisext
Council

Again, the doctrine is precisely that of the controversy of Caedmon's time, as closed towards the end of his time by the Quinisext Council. His dream begins with the splendours of a costly and brilliant cross, made of gold, adorned with gems, flashing in full beauty; no thing of shame; a thing so fair that angels gazed upon it. Then came the orthodox side, as though the Quinisext Council had broken in upon his dream with the words*, Sing "that the people may have their thoughts turned to His Passion and saving Death, and through His humiliation may learn His glory." A recent writer has remarked that the portions which appear on the Ruthwell Cross have been unskilfully selected. I venture to hold the exactly opposite view. The portions selected sound precisely the right note to any one who knows the ecclesiastical history of the time.

Oswald's
Cross

Again, when the sharp change comes in the course of the dream, and the Cross itself takes up the parable, we learn that it was a tree growing at the edge of a wood; it was cut down; men carried it on their shoulders, set it on a mound, fixed it there. I suggest that here the dream reproduces the exact details of the setting up of the wooden cross by Oswald on the day of his great victory some forty or more years before. They were details of which Caedmon had often heard, details kept perfectly vivid by the yearly pilgrimages to the spot where the actual cross still stood in Caedmon's time, the "victory-beacon" of the Bewcastle Cross its near neighbour.

On the whole, I am satisfied that if the words "Caedmon made me"

* See page 63.

are on the Ruthwell Cross, they tell us the exact truth of the portions of the poem that follow them.

Are those words on the Cross? I have a rubbing of runes on the head Caedmon
made me of the cross. Now a rubbing has this advantage over other methods, that it cannot shew marks of the leather where there is a groove on the stone. If there are grooves on the stone, there are corresponding blank places on the rubbing. They are rough in outline, if it is a much weathered inscription, but in characteristic letters the blank spaces are unmistakable. The ordinary rune for *g* for instance, a bold X, can scarcely be confused with any other rune. The same can be said of the ordinary rune *k*. Again, no other rune than *e* begins and ends as *e* does. Once more, the rune for *oe* leaves a fairly unmistakable blank, as does the rune for *đ* and *th*. The rune for *o* differs by a trifle from *a* and *ae*, and it is not easy to make a blank space which resembles one of these mean anything else than one of the three. The rune for *u* is unmistakable. See the table on p. 82.

Besides the rubbing taken at Ruthwell more than twenty-five years ago, I had four convincing squeezes taken at the same time. These squeezes were made up into a parcel to be sent to Professor Alois Brandl at Berlin, at that time a very sympathetic and friendly correspondent. The parcel was lost in my move from Bristol to London.

I shewed my rubbing last month to two friends well known in the Local pro-
nunciation world which knows about such things, at separate interviews. One of them opened our conversation with the frank statements (1) that the words are not on the cross, (2) that if they are there they have no meaning. Both of my friends agreed with me that the words can be read in the blank spaces shewn by the rubbing. One of the two, a first rate Anglo-Saxon scholar, told me in answer to a question that *fegan* was the word for 'to make a poem,' and he quoted the West Saxon *gefegde**. In answer to a request for a stronger verb, he gave me *fogan*, which would make, I suppose, *fogda*, pronounced broad. A slurred local pronunciation, taken down by some stranger to the locality, as the Norman inquisitors took down phonetically the names of places as given by unlettered Saxon witnesses and made sometimes a great mess of them, would soften the *d* into the *đ* of the inscription, and would soften the *g* into its frequent equivalent† *y*, and phonetically into a modified *o*. The name of Cedd's home, at a date previous to this, Ythancester, represented the great Roman fortress of Othona, the *y* and the initial *o* being pronounced as the *o* in our word

---

* King Alfred uses *gefegean* in this sense.

† In Northumbria we still call a gate a "yett." The quaint "Ayenbite of Inwyt" (1340), for "Remorse of Conscience," will be remembered.

'other.' My reading is †*kedmon mæ fauœda*. It is of course unnecessary for me to produce Anglo-Saxon examples of a monument or a work of art speaking of itself as 'me.' In other parts of this address I have noted examples of phonetic spelling.

Vietor's disproval

A recent writer has said that Vietor* completely disproved my reading, 'Kedmon.' I wondered what form this disproval would take. It begins with a suggestion that the first letter is R. In my judgment only a judicial blindness can make it other than K. Then he suggests D D Æ. Those are my D M͡O. On the other side he reads (F) A Y R Th O. Vietor's Y is an error. The rune looks rather like a modified U, but I long ago was convinced, and on examination I maintain the opinion, that the very deceptive mark of modification is merely a break in the stone. The U is a full inch broad at the bottom, and the break in the stone, the supposed modification mark, is in contact with the left member. The R is impossible; the lower part of it is the lower half of an X, the upper part forms a lozenge; the letter is *oe*; if only it had been an X, as the lower part suggests, we should have had our *fogda*. The O is not an O, the lower of the two side strokes has no upward turn; the stone is broken there; it is A. Five and twenty years ago I was wrong, with Vietor; I then read it as O.

Most of this is so fairly clear that a rubbing and a squeeze and a cast, taken as an interesting experiment from the great cast in the Victoria and Albert Museum by the kindness of Mr Maclagan and Mr Bedford, support me on each point, though of course that noble cast is not nearly as sharp as the original.

As to the runes for the name Cadmon or Caedmon or Cedmon, there is, after all, except for the initial R, not so much difference runically as to the English reader appears. The runes for D and M are very much alike; so are A and Æ and O and the first half of E; on a battered stone it is not easy to be quite sure as between N and Th. The following table shews the readings of six persons who have tried their hands at it. The table on p. 82 will shew the resemblances.

†Vietor	..	..	..	..	R		D	D	Æ	Th
Vigfusson and York Powell	..				K	S	D	M	A	
Sophus Bugge	..	..		..	G	O	D	M	O	N
Stephens..	..	..		..	K	A	D	M	O	N
G. F. Browne	..	..		..	K	E	D	M	O	N

---

* *Die Northumbrischen Runensteine*, Marburg in Hessen, 1895, p. 11.

† I have arranged Vietor's five suggestions in the six columns to which they seem to belong, and have omitted his brackets and query.

With so much agreement, it seems scarcely scientific to say that the six runes are absolutely illegible, or that Caedmon's name is not there.

It is a great pleasure to be able to add that though Vietor's eyes and fingers were unable to read what is fairly clear, his great learning and experience guided him to a definite opinion on the age of the Ruthwell Cross. In his opinion it cannot be put later than 750, that is, than Acca's and Ethelwold's crosses. It is a sore blow to the Davidian theory. Vietor's date

There remains a question of the spelling of the name. I read the runes as Kedmon, the *e* being I suppose so pronounced as to make 'Ked' rhyme with 'blade.' I was told nearly thirty years ago that this was a better form than Cadmon or Caedmon. Some one a few days ago said it was an impossible form. I see that of the four eighth century MSS. of Bede's Ecclesiastical History, one of the British Museum MSS. (Tiber. C. ii) and the Namur MS. agree in reading the first syllable as *cęd*. As there is so far as I know no other example of Caedmon's name in runes, my adversaries have not anything definite in rune knowledge to set against me. But I have something definite in rune knowledge to set against them. The spelling *Kedmon*

Few things have struck me more in the long but hopelessly interrupted course of investigations of details of those very early times, than the curious way in which any little things we do know support or illustrate one another. One would probably say that if the name of the king who reigned in the later part of Caedmon's life, Aldfrith, was put into runes, it would begin with some definite form of A. But the king's moneyer knew better. On the only coin of King Aldfrith which I know, the 'Aldfridus' has in place of an A the same unmistakable rune for *e* that I read in the Ruthwell Kedmon. It is the only rune on the coin. It may be added that one authority gives his name as Ealdferth. But while I abide by my reading *Kedmon*, I am willing to acquiesce in a verdict by real experts in favour of some other spelling of our sacred poet's name on the Cross.

Professor Cook writes at some length on Drahmal's Cross, at Ste Gudule, Brussels, which has some words on it taken in the main from the Dream of the Rood. This was discovered and published in 1891 by Dr Logeman, who represented English philology in the University of Ghent. He sent me a copy of his publication and lent me his original photographs, which I published in my *St Aldhelm*. I lectured on the Cross here on April 26, 1892. It is a beautiful piece of English silver-work, with *Drahmal me worhte* incised upon it in very dainty letters. Professor Cook has misunderstood the position of the actual inscription. It is riveted on to the thin edges of the cross, running up one edge from the foot, round the Drahmal's Cross

arms and head, and down to the foot on the other side. The reading which
I printed in my syllabus for 1892 was as follows:— † Rod is min nama geo
ic ricne cyning bær byfigynde blode bestemed thas rode het Æthlmær
wyrican ꝸ Aðelwold* hys berotho Criste to lofe for Ælfrices saule hyra
berothor.

This is not the form, nor the wording, nor the spelling, of the Ruthwell
Cross or of the Vercelli Dream of the Rood. It is evident that the beautiful
poem was known to the brothers, and they used such parts of it as they
pleased, in the spelling of their time, and in their own words. Professor
Skeat told me that it was the ordinary spelling of about 1050 and could
not be far before or after that date or the Norman Conquest†. The use
to which Professor Cook puts this as an argument in connection with his
twelfth century theory is rather curious. "The Brussels inscription
indicates that *The Dream of the Rood* was drawn upon in the 11th or 12th
century for epigraphic purposes, and therefore tends to confirm any independent presumption that the Ruthwell Cross inscription is to be assigned
to a late period, or at least does nothing to invalidate such a presumption."
It may be added that the Alfred Jewel bears the legend † *Ælfred mec
heht gewyrican.*

The Anglo-Saxon Chronicle has the names of these three brothers in
the years 982, 983, 984, but not as related to one another. They were
personages. The Aldorman Æthelmær died in 982. Æthelwold the
bishop of Winchester died in 984. It would not be in accordance with the
practice of the Chronicle to state that he was Æthelmær's brother if the
fact was so. Ælfric became aldorman in 983, and was driven out of the
country in 985. He was known as "Ælfric child," and in Latin as
"cognomento puer." There seems to be no reason why the two older
men should not have had this valuable cross made as an offering for their
younger brother Ælfric's spiritual welfare while he was yet alive, in a time
and in a position of many and great dangers‡. He may have taken it to
Flanders when he fled. I have suggested elsewhere that it came into the
possession of Archbishop Egbert of Trèves, who was the son of the Count
of Flanders of that period, 963–988. I cannot see that it has any sort of
connection with the date of the Ruthwell Cross.

* Professor Cook justly remarks that the photograph does not shew an aspirated D.
Dr Logeman says it is aspirated. Photographs are not infallible guides to the truth in
inscriptions.

† See more in my *St Aldhelm*, p. 196.

‡ In the Isle of Man people were putting up crosses with runic inscriptions (in Manx
runes and language) for their own soul and for the souls of living relatives. In 982, Dorset-
shire was ravaged by Vikings, and London was burned.

Something must be said of objections to the reading of the Bewcastle runes on philological grounds, though I do not profess any competence to do more than suggest in such a matter.

I am told by critics of the main inscription that the Anglo-Saxon *The word* for 'thin,' 'slender,' is *thynne*, and there is no such word in Anglo-Saxon as *thun* *thun*. I reply that there is such a word, and that it occurs in the very earliest piece of Anglo-Saxon prose which we have in the original; it occurs on the Bewcastle Cross. *Thynne* is all very well for fully developed Anglo-Saxon, but on the face of it it is a developed word. The steps of the development are simple, but they took time. The *y* is a modified *u*. The modified *u* comes from a full *u*. Thus we get the word back to the form in all the kindred languages of the time. Our word *thynne* stands alone in its disuse of *u*. The modern German keeps the modified *u*, *dünn*. I am aware that a second *n*, as the relic of a second syllable, is not un-important.

Professor Cook does not state the case against *thun* quite fairly. He remarks that there is no Old English word *thun*; the nearest approach to it is *đyn(ne)*, *đin(ne)*, 'thin.' But why does Professor Cook create a difference which does not exist? He prints the Bewcastle word as *thun* and the Old English word as *đynne*. But the initial letter is the same in each case, a softened *d*. Print the Bewcastle word as *đun* or the Old English word as *thynne*, and the connection is clear.

Thus the attack on the word *thun* as non-existent at Bewcastle, because not an Anglo-Saxon word, brings out the fact that it is a strong evidence of great earliness of date. I may add that after all there is such a word in Anglo-Saxon. It comes in composition with *wang*, 'the cheek.' *Thun-wang* is the 'temple,' 'the thin-cheek.' So I am assured on high authority.

If we set out with the principle that each word on the Bewcastle Cross *The word* must be in completely regular form, and used in a completely regular *æft* manner, meaning, by 'regular,' in accordance with the grammatical development of the Old English language, the word *aft* or *æft* is no doubt a difficulty. Its form and its use are two separate questions. As to its use, the word means 'behind,' and the experts tell us that it is only on memorial stones that it is used as meaning 'in memory of.' They do not tell us by what other very short phrase that meaning could be conveyed in the laborious task of cutting letters on hard stone. So much as this is certain, that some one used it for the first time in this sense, and that the some one was not guided by any form of Latin memorial phrase. It is of solely lapidary use, and it seems singularly well fitted for such use.

Professor Cook finds it in inscriptions on Manx stones, which he dates 1050 to 1100, in both forms *aft* and *aftir*, and he therefore takes that arbitrary date as the "*terminus a quo* for all the English stones bearing *æft* or *æfter* in this sense." This is an extraordinary induction. The Manx inscriptions are not in Old English. There is not on the Bewcastle shaft any connection with the Manx tongue, the script is very different, so is the ornamentation. I gave to my class in 1891 practically all the main Manx inscriptions, and that they might be read by persons who only knew the Anglian runes I gave them a table of the Manx runes, ten of which are not the same as the Anglian runes. As for language, what sort of connection is there between the Bewcastle ...*setton this sigbekn thun æft Alkfrithu*, and the Manx ...*raisti krus thona aftir Arinbiaurk*? And why should the evidently modern Manx be taken as a *terminus a quo* for purely English stones, rather than the evidently ancient Old English?

As regards the form *aft* or *æft*, in place of *æfter* which the experts tell us is philologically the earlier form, it is here that difficulty is said to come in. I do not remember another case of its use. One of the Thornhill inscriptions has the form *æfte*, I think without the final *r*; otherwise we have *æfter*. The Collingham inscription has *æftar Onsuini ku* , and this is possibly even earlier than 670. Bede gives us a delightful account of the charms of the young King Oswin who ruled Deira from 644 to 651 when he was slain by Oswy under specially cruel circumstances. He was a friend of Bishop Aidan, evidently a man to whom, in the Upton* phrase, the 'folk' might well have 'raised a beacon' at the grave-mound. There is a curious hint that the name Oswin had some other letter in the first syllable; it became Oisin† in Ireland. We have a beautiful little stone which bears the two names Oswin and Tondhere, the one faithful soldier who was slain with him. We do not know of any other king whom the Collingham Cross can have commemorated. The omission of the nasal *n* which converts Anlaf and Onlaf into Olaf and Olave will be borne in mind.

I should myself be satisfied with an appeal to the probability of local use, or of mere irregularity, as accounting for *æft* at so early a date as 670. But we have a better answer to the objectors than that. The late Dr Skeat, once our distinguished Professor of Anglo-Saxon, whose Etymological Dictionary of the English Language is a monument of cautious work, has the following remark under the head *Aft, After*, "In English, there has, no doubt, been from the very first a feeling that *after* was formed from *aft*; but comparative philology shews at once that this is merely an English view, and due to a mistake. The word *aft* is, in fact, an abbreviation

---

* Upton in Wirrall.
† The same word as Ossian we are told.

or development from *after*, which is the older word of the two, and the only form found in most other languages." I would emphasise Dr Skeat's phrase *from the very first*. Professor Cook will scarcely claim 1050–1100 as Dr Skeat's *terminus a quo*.

It may be added that here as in so many of the cases of dispute raised by Professor Cook, David's position is weaker than Alchfrith's.

Bosworth may be out of date as an expert authority on Anglo-Saxon spelling and grammar. But I do not think any one will call in question the correctness of his remarks on the great irregularity of usage evidenced by Anglo-Saxon manuscripts. He speaks* of the discrepancies in the forms of words which occur in nearly every page of an Anglo-Saxon author. Not writing by established rules of grammar often arbitrary, the author wrote just as he spoke. His writing was therefore the true representative of his dialect. Another cause of irregularity lay in the diphthongal nature of Anglo-Saxon vowels. This made it difficult to know by what letters to indicate the proper sounds of his words. He often interchanged kindred vowels in the same word, at one time *a* or *éo*, and afterwards *æ* and *y*.

Irregularity in Anglo-Saxon MSS.

These observations tend to support my contention that some at least of the difficulties found at Bewcastle and Ruthwell by exact and rigid scholars who demand that everything is to be rejected which is not according to a rule developed in an advanced age, are merely matters of local usage, sometimes of local pronunciation, in an early age, where irregularities were the rule not the exception. I have no idea how the rune-cutter would pronounce the word *fauœđa*. But I do know that the three words of which it is one are, so far as we know, the only words on the cross which are not quotation from a manuscript. They are the one phrase that is put down as spoken, probably by some one who spoke very broad Northumbrian. I need scarcely point out that the more Professor Cook presses the impossibility of there being any meaning in the words as they appear in runes, the deeper he is cutting the throat of his theory that they were incised when Anglo-Saxon had passed through some centuries of existence as a literary language, and sculptors were under literary management.

A recognition of the common-sense view enunciated by Bosworth would have saved a great deal of time and imagination which has been spent on the word *Cyniburug* by Professor Cook and Dr Hewison. It is simply *Cyniburg* pronounced with a Northumbrian burr. An apt parallel is found in two examples of various readings of the name Alchfrith in the Life of Wilfrith by Eddi. It is specially interesting to note that in each case it is in the heading of a chapter, not in Eddi's text, a difference akin

Local pronunciation

* *Anglo-Saxon Dictionary*, 1838. *Preface*, p. xxvii.

to the position of the Kedmon phrase in relation to the text of the Dream. Of the two main manuscripts of Eddi's Life, one has a special connection with Northumbria; it spells Alchfrith *Aluchfrith*.

Another Bewcastle example is *ean*, for *one*. Professor Cook briefly says* "There is no *ean* in Old English." *Ean* is merely phonetic. It has never changed its sound in Northumbria. The hostile writer goes to Scotland, and finds *ane* used for 'one.' Why not try the true locality, Northumbria? If you ask a man who has all but sold out his stock, how many he has left, if he is a real Northumbrian he will tell you—to quicken your intention to purchase—nobbut yan†. Lul, the successor of Boniface in the See of Mainz, wrote in one of his epistles the names of the runes, in the order of the English alphabet—so to call it. When he comes to the name of the rune for *y*, he spells it *ian*.

Another example of local pronunciation appears in the Bewcastle *bekn*, pronounced short and sharp. This we find in later sepulchral runic inscriptions as *bekun*; *folkæ arærdon bekun* at Upton, *bekun at bergi* at Thornhill.

Gessus Kristtus

It seems curious that Professor Cook has ignored the remarkable evidence of the †*Gessus Kristtus* at Bewcastle, in his notes on this phrase. In writing on it he says (p. 249) "The only perfect parallels to this with which I am acquainted are to be found on the censers from Hesselager and Kullerup, in Denmark. The former reads in runes *Gesus Krist*, and the latter †*Gesus Krt*." These are very far indeed from being perfect parallels. There is none of the reduplication of consonants in the first word which appears to point to local pronunciation at Bewcastle, as does the remarkable *tus* of which Professor Cook makes here no count. These reduplications remind one of the same feature carried to excess in the curious Ogam inscriptions of the Pictish part of Caledonia. He adds that "the spelling *Gesus*, according to the highest authority on the subject, Professor Wimmer, was a customary spelling at this period [the period of the censers], the latest years of the 13th century." As there is no special rune for J, I should be surprised if *Jesus* were otherwise spelled in runes. Our words 'year' and 'yea' were spelled in ordinary script *gear* and *gae* in Anglo-Saxon. The special point at Bewcastle is that the name is spelled *Gessus*, not that it is spelled *Gesus*.

---

* *Bewcastle Cross*, p. 144.

† We used to torment my poultry-loving mother when we were boys by singing

> I'll gang yam, and tell my mam,
> 'At all oor geese is deead but yan,
> An' it's a steg, wi' oot a leg,
> An' it'll be deead afore a gets yam.

Professor Cook says a good deal about the word *Cynnburug*, arguing about the form of its two parts, Cynn and burug, with a view to prove that neither is so old as 670. Dr Hewison, on the other hand, thinks that it may have been the original Anglian name of Bewcastle, as though a "royal borough." Bede's Latin form is Cyniburga*. The double *n*, if it is fully pronounced, involves a sound which suits Bede's form; and the second *n* is not improbably an *i*. But enough has been said already about these confident assertions based on the assumption that philological accuracy was achieved by the designers or sculptors of these ancient monuments. We have the pronunciation of the name of Alchfrith's widow in common use to-day. She is still a living personage to the people of Castor near Peterborough, where she founded the abbey over which she presided, with her sister Cyneswitha a professed nun under or with her. A ridge way in Castor Field is to this day called "Lady Cunnyburrow's Way." She and Cyneswitha cannot be explained away, any more than Alchfrith and Ecgfrith and Wulfhere and Oswy can. With regard to the spelling at the end of the word, it is, as I have said, only another example of phonetic spelling. The Northumbrian of to-day would certainly pronounce Kyniburg with a rolled *r*, as no doubt the Northumbrian of 670 did.

Professor Cook, in dealing with the curious word on the Ruthwell Cross which he reads as *ungget*, writes thus (p. 246), "It looks as though the sculptor had carved a word whose spelling was unfamiliar to him and had done it bunglingly."

I will take this opportunity of suggesting to some critics that at Bewcastle we have the original edition of the inscriptions, absolutely unchanged from the moment they were incised on the stone. That is not the case with any Anglo-Saxon manuscript with which I am acquainted, of the date we assign to the inscriptions. The critics base their comparative criticisms on Anglo-Saxon manuscripts copied by one generation from the work of a previous generation, itself in turn copied from a still earlier original. The first edition does not so far as I know in any case go back to our date. Criticism of an inscription cut in 670, and untouched since, based on forms found in comparatively late manuscripts as altered by one copyist after another, is not scientific. The faults found are there because they have not been edited by later people. Criticisms of this character are arguments for the early date.

I do not anywhere suggest in explanation of a difficulty that the designer or the sculptor made a grammatical mistake or used a wrong

Marginal note: Cynnburug

Marginal note: Mistakes

---

* *H.E.* iii. 21.

Mistakes   rune. But it is always at the back of one's mind that if what is in all its other features clear is spoiled by some one such detail as the presence or the absence of about half-an-inch of incision, the incisor may conceivably not have been absolutely infallible. I attended some four years ago the unveiling of a great Scottish monument by a great Scottish Duke in honour of a highly respected laird. I had been asked to inspect it the day before, to examine the Scottish ornamentation. On the whole it was very fair, just one detail not of the first class. But in the ordinary English of the rather long inscription there were two mistakes, and one of them was an actual mistake in spelling. Why are we to assume that no incisor in Scotland in 685 could have put the rune *g* in place of *c* in *gesceaft*, if in 1912, this highly critical century, under ducal patronage, an incisor in that very same Scotland made a much worse mistake, if indeed the wrong rune is to be classed as a mere mistake, which I do not allow? There is a runic mistake in one sepulchral inscription, and it is evident on the face of it, for quaintly enough the rune-cutter openly corrected it. In the name Hildigith he left out the *g*, whereupon he drilled a hole between the *i* and the *i* and above the line cut a large ✕ for *g*. But there again, was it a mere mistake? Was it not the case that no one really pronounced the *g* in the name of the Hartlepool nun, and the sculptor cut the name exactly as he knew it, and the Prioress, probably Hild herself, afterwards Hilda of Whitby, made him insert the practically mute *g*? That is another example of a local illustration before rather than after our period 670–685.

Doubtful runes   Doubt has been cast upon the earliness of two of the runes used at Bewcastle, ᚸ and ᛣ for ✕ and ᚲ, that is, for *g* and *k*. I should naturally reply that this is their first appearance. They must have appeared for the first time somewhere, and at Bewcastle we are dealing with workmen of initiative impulse. And I do not see reason for assigning to them, in their first appearance, a force different from the force of the runes which they replace. My explanation of them here is that they are purely decorative. The manuscript school of Northumbria, at that early period, avoided blank spaces in a line of letters on a decorative page, and rejoiced in capital letters. At Bewcastle, the ✕ is broad, not slender, and if left to itself it would make a triangular gap on each side. The sculptor occupied this by the fourth part of the circumference of a circle, giving a curved line, which was quite alien from the principle of a runic letter and therefore no part of a rune proper. As to its being a guttural *g*, I do not find any other *g* at Bewcastle, and so far as I know what the word guttural means, a guttural *g* is not specially required in some at least of the cases of its use. The runes at Ruthwell are more slender, less broad, and there we find the ordinary *g*. Inasmuch as the Bewcastle Cross was, on our theory, the first great runic monument set up in Christian England, and we have the evidence of Pada's Coin* that very special attention was paid shortly before its erection to the production of beautiful runes, I feel that we are entitled to take into consideration the idea of something decorative and grandiose in the purpose of the designers of the shaft and its inscriptions.

In ᚻ the decorative idea is evident, but with it I cannot help feeling that the idea of capital letters is concerned. As in the other case a curved

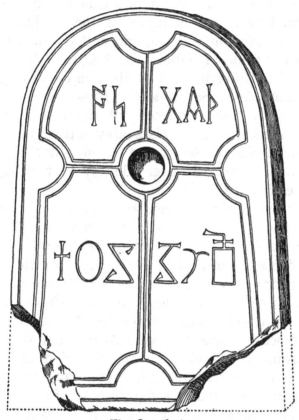

e. The Osgyð stone.

line is used, contrary to runic usage, so here a horizontal line is employed, of which there is no example in the true futhork, the reason being that you cannot handily cut horizontal lines on a tally of splintering Baltic deal. It is simply the doubled *k* which we find in the first letter of *Christ* on the Bewcastle Cross, cut square, and with a cross line to occupy spaces which would otherwise have been awkward gaps. We have discovered a curious parallel to this on a pillow-stone from Lindisfarne, with the name *Osgyð* in runes and in capitals. The *ð* in capitals is a large rectangular

* See page 30.

D, with a little cross at the top as in ⊞; it is shewn in figure *e*, which I owe to the Society of Antiquaries of London. The ornamental letter ⊞ is only used as an initial letter, and only in the words *Christ, King,* and the names of two royal ladies. It is a glorified initial K. The suggestion of an initial letter has of course less weight than the suggestion of the treatment of ✕ on the principle of occupying gaps.

Later runes   Professor Baldwin Brown and Mr O. M. Dalton are naturally disturbed by the evidence of later date of these two runes. Professor von Freising of Upsala, "one of the very foremost runic scholars of the day," has informed Professor Baldwin Brown that he agrees in the attribution to the famous Alcuin, a scholar of Northumbrian origin and training, of the "Salzburg MS.," which gives a runic alphabet something like that on the Thames Sword in the British Museum, without the five later characters which are given in subsequent Anglo-Saxon MSS. These five later characters, he adds, were apparently not introduced till about the middle of the 9th century, and two of them occur unmistakably in the runes on the Bewcastle Cross. At the same time Professor von Freising does not think that this runic argument need necessarily over-ride any very strong archaeological evidence for an earlier date.

The identification of the Salzburg MS. with Alcuin is not a very strong peg on which to hang the displacing of the Bewcastle Cross from the 7th century and the placing it after the middle of the 9th, a period at which we have no evidence of any large continuance of the use of runes in Northumbria, especially on what must have been one of the very noblest monuments of its age whatever that age was. Unfortunately I was not shewn this manuscript at Salzburg when the Abbat there shewed me all that I wanted to see in connection with Alcuin, nor was it mentioned to me*. I was writing the life of this distinguished head master of my old school at York, and the visit to Salzburg was one part of my preparation for the work. I may add that for the purpose of my book I read all of Alcuin's letters, and translated many of them. I was very much on the look out for any mention of runes, and I did not find any. The complete absence—so far as I could see—of such mention, appeared to me to be an argument against their use on a great monument, as the only script, at any period considerably later than that with which we are concerned.

It appears that the later Anglo-Saxon MSS. give these two letters and three others at the end of the regular futhork. Their absence from that position in the supposed Alcuin futhork, is taken as serious evidence that they were not in use in Alcuin's time. In that view I cannot acquiesce,

* Probably the reference is to a Salzburg MS. at Vienna on which Grimm wrote; that futhork is given by Stephens, i. 102; he mentions its supposed connection with Arno, Alcuin's friend.

unless the list is prefaced by words which shew that the writer believed The Salzburg runes those to be the only runes in existence. I can well understand a purist like Alcuin giving the whole of the ancient futhork and not allowing a place to alternative forms. The modified *u* for example, ⑴, is a common rune, but I do not find it given in any futhork. I may add that I have not been able to find the exact ⋈ and the exact ⊕ of Bewcastle in any of the Anglo-Saxon MSS. quoted by Stephens. The example set at Bewcastle of occupying void spaces by the insertion of curves in the angles of the *g* rune is carried much further. The four extremities of the rune are fitted with streamers, and the centre is occupied by a lozenge. The *k* rune is made non-symmetrical by the insertion of a streamer at the left of the top, as in the uncial *đ* on the Osgyđ stone on page 79, the balancing cross line being omitted. In each case the parent is much superior to the offspring.

We have a letter from Lul of Malmesbury, Archbishop of Mainz in Lul's runic alphabet succession to our great missionary bishop Boniface, and a correspondent of Cuthbert, Abbat of Wearmouth, in which the names of the runes are given but not the runes themselves*. Lul's letters are of an intimate and affectionate character†, and it may be that he learned something about the Anglian runes by letter from Northumbria. But his connection with Wearmouth was probably much more close than that, for it would appear that he and Burchardt of Würzburg finished their studies at Wearmouth after leaving Malmesbury‡. The curious point about Lul's list of the names of the runes is that he arranges them in the order of our abc, or alphabet as we call it as though it were Greek, not in the order of the runic futhork, f, u, th, o, r, k. He begins with asc, berc, can; he has a rune name for each of our letters, *i* and *u* including *j* and *v*, and *wen* for *w* being omitted; he ends with ilc, ian, zar, for *x, y, z*. The list comes among a number of queer things at the end of the letter, such as R. R. R., P. P. P., etc.§, the puzzle which according to one veracious history Bede interpreted at Rome, thus earning from the Senate of Rome the title of Venerable!‖ This collocation naturally gives the impression that the Anglian runes had ceased to be a script for dignified purposes, and had become things to toy with in literary circles. Lul's letter is before 755, when Alcuin was still a student at the archiepiscopal School of York. The silence of Bede on the subject of runes seems to point in the same

---

* *Epistolae Merowingici et Karolini aevi*, Berlin, 1892, vol. I, p. 384. It is vol. III of the *Monumenta Germaniae Historica*, Berolini, apud Weidemannos, 1892.

† See my *Boniface of Crediton* for the letters to and from Cuthbert, pp. 296–302.

‡ *Boniface of Crediton*, pp. 139, 140, 303.

§ See my *Venerable Bede*, page 21.

‖ Rex Romanorum Ruit, Pater Patriae Profectus est, etc.

direction.   Runes were still in use for short inscriptions on tombstones, as at Thornhill in the West Riding of Yorkshire.   The Danes, who did so much to destroy the literature and the monuments of the Anglo-Saxons, eventually introduced the Scandinavian runes, but only on a small scale. The more we look into these matters, the more hopeless does a 12th century date become for such monuments as the Bewcastle and Ruthwell Crosses.

A table of Anglian runes in the order of the futhork is appended, as given by Isaac Taylor in his *Greeks and Goths* (Macmillan, 1879) at page 55.   Those in the third line do not find a place in the futhork, but the first three of them are of continual occurrence in early times. I am disinclined to attach very serious importance to the omission of an alternative or a supplementary rune from a manuscript futhork.   We sometimes argue about such things as though an Anglo-Saxon writer had had access to the students' room of the British Museum.

CHAPTER VII

Alchfrith and Aldfrith.—Dr Hewison's arguments.—Stephen Eddi.—Bede.—Fridegoda.—The Anglo-Saxon Chronicle.—Florence of Worcester.—William of Malmesbury.—Cyniburg and Cuthburg.—Concluding remarks.

In order to get rid of the difficulty of Alchfrith's name being found— though "in feminine case"—on the Bewcastle Cross, Dr Hewison sets out to shew that there was no such person as "the mysterious prince of Bewcastle," Alchfrith, "sub-king of Deira."

First he declares that the name on the cross, which he renders as Alcfrith, was not anciently and usually so written. It was Alchfrid, Alhfrid, Alhfriđ, never Alcfrith or Alkfrith. Take the first syllable. He reads it *Alc* on the cross, and objects that it was *Alch*, and then *Alh*, never *Alc* or *Alk*. He forgets that he is dealing with a rune. There is only one rune for *c ch* and *k*; he has no more right to say it is *Alc* on the cross than others have to say, if they wish, that it is *Alch*. In accordance with the consistent spelling of Eddi and Bede, the runic spelling is correct. Take the second syllable. *Friđ* is right, we are told, the *frith* of the cross is wrong. But again he forgets that he is dealing with a rune. There is only one rune for *dh* and *th*, and if *dh* is the right spelling, that is the spelling of the cross, if *th* is right, that is the spelling of the cross. On his own shewing, the cross is right in both syllables, as far as runes can make it right.

The name Alchfrith

Then he maintains that Alchfrith and King Aldfrith are one and the same person. In the life of Wilfrith by his intimate friend Stephen Eddi, Alchfrith, the son of Oswy and joint king with Oswy, played a very important part in the early life of Wilfrith, down to the synod of Whitby in 664. Eddi certainly knew all about Alchfrith, very much more than he tells us; for he, like Bede, makes no mention of Alchfrith's acts after 664. It is one of the mysteries of our history. Now Eddi always spells him Alchfrith. The one case of *Alhfrith*, which Dr Hewison quotes, is not in the text, it is in the heading of chs. VII and VIII, and thus not by Eddi's unwavering hand, with the very drastic various reading Aluchfrid, an interesting and valuable record of pronunciation.

Alchfrith and Aldfrith

From chapter VIII with its Alchfrith, prior to 664, Eddi drops him. We then pass on to ch. XLIV, a space of more than twenty years, to the death of King Ecgfrith, the disappeared Alchfrith's brother, to whom Eddi tells us that Aldfrith succeeded. The next fifteen chapters have plenty to say of Aldfrith down to his death in 705. He is always Aldfrith in the text, as his oldest half-brother, all those years before, is always Alchfrith. They were to Eddi, who knew perfectly what he was doing, certainly two different men. Eddi continues the life of his friend Wilfrith to his death in 709, when Aldfrith had been dead for some years.

The same features appear in the Ecclesiastical History of Bede, who tells us more about Alchfrith and Aldfrith than Eddi does. Those are his names for them, and he has exactly the same long gap between them that Eddi has. Bede remarks of Aldfrith that he was "said to be" the son of Oswy and brother of Ecgfrith, while, some twenty-five years before, he had described Oswy and his son Alchfrith—of whose paternity no doubt is suggested—as going on a campaign together. We are asked to believe that Alchfrith and Aldfrith are one and the same man.

But the Ecclesiastical History is not Bede's only historical work. We shall find Aldfrith, and entirely to our purpose, in his History of St Cuthbert. It is a pretty little story. It explains Bede's remark that Aldfrith was "said to be" a brother of his predecessor Ecgfrith, Oswy's son and successor. This is the story. The Abbess Ælflæd, of Whitby, the sister of Ecgfrith and half-sister of Alchfrith, the princess who was born in 654 and was vowed to God in her infancy by her father Oswy as a thank-offering for a great victory won by him and his son Alchfrith, became very anxious in 684 to know who would succeed to the kingdom on the death of her brother Ecgfrith*, who "had neither sons nor brothers." The death took place in the next year. She entreated St Cuthbert, who visited her on Coquet isle, to tell her what would happen. He said: "Behold this great sea, how it aboundeth in islands. It is easy for God out of some of these to provide a person to reign over the Angles." She understood him to speak of Alfrid, who was said to be the son of her father and was then living in the isles of the Scots (Ireland) from love of learning. But she knew that her brother Ecgfrith meant to make him a bishop. This was the illegitimate son of Oswy, who succeeded in the next year. We are asked to believe that Alchfrith and he were one and the same. Aldfrith was one of the most learned men of his time; devoted to literature and art; a correspondent, under the name of Acircius, of my predecessor Aldhelm of Malmesbury †.

Now these abundant evidences of the separate existence of a sub-king Alchfrith who is last heard of in connection with the council of Whitby

---

* cum filiis careret et fratribus.

† See my *St Aldhelm*, pp. 304–8.

and a sole king Aldfrith who reigned from 685 to 705, taken from Eddi and Bede, are as nothing to Dr Hewison in comparison with the statements of non-contemporary writers—it may be noted by the way that Dr Hewison says* Bede was only eight years old when Aldfrith became king in 685, but according to accepted dates he was twelve or thirteen. Dr Hewison remarks among objections to the separate existence of Alchfrith that "in the Liber Vitæ (ninth century) appear Alchfrith and Altfrith." So they do, and on the face of it as two separate kings. But the evidence of the Liber Vitæ is in detail strongly against Dr Hewison. The list of kings who were enrolled in the Lindisfarne and Durham Book of Life, to be remembered in eucharistic services, begins with Edwin and Oswald. The next four names are Osuio, Ecgfrith, Alchfrith, Aelfuini, that is king Oswy, his son who succeeded him, and his two sons whom we know to have been sub-kings with him. Then come seven names, not of Northumbrian kings. Then, thus marked off, Altfrith, that is king Aldfrith, certainly not a repetition of a name nine places above, and then we come to Eadwulf, who succeeded Aldfrith for a time, and Coenred Osred and Osric the three following kings. What comfort those who deny the separate existence of Alchfrith find in that, it is not easy to see. Another objection is that in the list of kings appended to Bede, Aldfrid, not Alchfrid, is included; the reason is obvious, the sub-king Alchfrith did not reign over the kingdom of Northumbria. Again, "in Fridegoda's Life† (tenth century) we find Alhfridus (Alfridus)." So we do, but Fridegoda—we are getting a little late in the search for evidence to correct Eddi and Bede,—is quite clear against his quoter who calls him as a witness. At the beginning of Wilfrith's life as a Northumbrian ecclesiastic, Fridegoda says the twin kings...*gemelli, Alhfridus imperitans una genitor simul Oswiu*, received him and he was given Ripon. If Dr Hewison had read on, he would have found at the other end of Wilfrith's life, after Oswy and Alchfrith had long disappeared, that when *Ekfridus* was slain *Aldfridus* succeeded, and *Aldfridus* recalled Wilfrith. There are other spellings and variations, but Fridegoda never returns to the Alhfridus of Wilfrith's early years. He is clear against Dr Hewison.

As to who Aldfrith's wife was, the Anglo-Saxon Chronicle quite possibly knew what it was about when it made its only entrance on the subject. The occasion was the death of Ingild, the brother of Ini king of Wessex, in 718. "Their sisters were Cwenburh and Cuthburh. And Cuthburh "raised the monastery at Wimborne. And she was given to Ealdferth

* Probably misled by the error of Florence of Worcester, 'A. 678,' corrected in the *Monumenta Hist. Brit.* p. 535, *Natus est Beda*, A. 673. Florence erroneously describes him as *Sanctus Beda*.

† of Wilfrith.

"king of the Northumbrians, but they separated during his life." In this the five best MSS. of the Anglo-Saxon Chronicle exactly agree, except that the best of the five spells his name Aldferth and hers both Cuthburh and Cuthburg.

Dr Hewison quotes some modern writers of repute who treat Alchfrith and Aldfrith as one and the same person. They cannot be called authoritative improvers of Eddi and Bede in a matter very familiar to those first-hand historians. They would be the last to claim such a position.

Of course they had what appeared to them to be an early authority for this identity. The source of their statements can be found in William of Malmesbury, whom Dr Hewison claims as his authority too, in concert with Florence of Worcester. To those 12th century authorities we must therefore turn*.

Florence of Worcester and William of Malmesbury were writing their histories about the same time, early in the 12th century. Florence is supposed to have died about 1118, William about 1143†. Florence tells us that Oswy with his son Alhfrid conquered the Mercians; that the kings Oswy and Alhfrid his son who had succeeded to the kingdom of Oithilwald, Oswald's son, were at the synod of Whitby; that Eata founded Ripon at the request of King Alhfrid; and that King Alhfrid, with the advice and consent of his father Oswy, sent Wilfrid to the king of the Galliæ to be consecrated. Florence drops Alhfrid the sub-king entirely, from the mention of Wilfrid's consecration in 664, as do Bede and Eddi. He makes no reference to any illegitimacy, or to any rejection at the time when Ecgfrith succeeded Oswy. In 685, twenty-one years later, he says that on the death of Ecgfrith, "Alhfrid his brother succeeded, a man most learned in the Scriptures." It seems impossible that he took this brother to be the same as the one he had so freely mentioned during a considerable period all those years before, and yet did not refer to what would, if it were true, be a very remarkable fact, namely, his succession to Ecgfrith, after having not succeeded Oswy. However that may be, he did not spell correctly the name of King Aldfrith in its most important letter. But he makes up for that later on by informing us that 'Aldfrith' King of the Northumbrians had to wife Cuthburh, quoting the passage from the Anglo-Saxon Chronicle already given.

The Alchfrith of Eddi and Bede, the sub-king who with his father Oswy

* Dr Hewison mentions a little work of this same late period, supposed to be by Symeon of Durham (1130), where 'Alcfrid' is said to have succeeded Ecgfrid.

† The abbeys of Worcester and Malmesbury were very closely connected. It was the Bishop of Worcester who conducted the ceremonies of the funeral of Aldhelm of Malmesbury in 709. Florence and William were probably in personal communication.

conquered the Mercians, married Cyniburga, the daughter of Penda, the Mercian king, about 660. Dr Hewison writes, "William of Malmesbury "states that Aldfrith (not Alchfrith) being illegitimate and an elder son "succeeded the younger Ecfrid legitimately born, and married Kineburga: "*De Gestis Reg. Angl.* edit. Stubbs, i. 57, 58." William describes Oswy's acts, military and ecclesiastical, without any reference to a son. When he died, he left two sons, the younger legitimate, who succeeded, the elder, being illegitimate, was barred*. William does not name him. Then we come to the entry, 'the death of Egfrid came to the ears of his brother Alfrid who had been rejected as illegitimate and had lived in Ireland,' and he succeeded.

William tells us † (p. 35) that Ina of the West Saxons had two sisters, one of whom, Cuthburga, was married to Alfrid king of the Northumbrians. Then he tells us (p. 78 ‡), that Alfrid king of the Northumbrians married Kineburga, the daughter of Penda, but she left him and went to her monastery. It was certainly not a "king of the Northumbrians" that married Kineburga, it was a sub-king.

It was very easy for William to confuse two names so much alike in some of their spellings as these two were. And it may be said that Alchfrith was the son of a princess of the British kingdom of Rheged, and that might possibly make his mother's marriage questionable, sufficiently to found some idea of non-succession to the throne. Enough has been said to shew that Eddi and Bede had no confusion as between the two.

When we look more closely into the position of Eddi and Bede, it seems rather absurd to reject them in favour of William of Malmesbury. Eddi was in Wilfrith's service for forty years; he was frequently with him; his opportunities of observation were considerable. He had at his command the knowledge of Tatberht, who urged upon him the undertaking of the work. Tatberht was Wilfrith's kinsman and constant companion, whom he appointed Provost of Ripon. In the pathetic chapter (LXIV) in which Eddi tells of Wilfrith's death at Oundle, he informs us that in view of his approaching death Wilfrith related to his kinsman Tatberht the whole course of his life as they rode together. Acca, too, Wilfrith's friend and successor and Bede's correspondent, had much to tell his biographer. Finally, it is certain that Eddi had access to the letters and documents connected with the great controversies which had so seriously spoiled his

* Factione optimatum, quamvis senior.
† This is in the "first recension." The complications of the recensions, and of the incorporations of William's history into Florence or his continuator, are very puzzling.
‡ Dr Hewison's reference for the marriage is wrong.

master's life and work.   It seems impossible that Eddi could have avoided
the obvious remark that King Aldfrith was Wilfrith's old friend and patron
Alchfrith, especially considering that Aldfrith was dead and gone some
years before Wilfrith died, and his boy son was of no account, if indeed
he too had not passed away and been succeeded by a fifth cousin once
removed.   There was certainly no political danger in a remark that
Aldfrith was Alchfrith, if it had been true.   It may be added that Eddi
had special reason to know about Alchfrith's relations with Wilfrith, for
Eddi went north with Wilfrith in 669 to teach music, just at the time when
Alchfrith's mysterious disappearance had taken place or was taking place.

Eddi's Life of Wilfrith is the beginning of the Ecclesiastical History
of the English, having precedence of Bede by a considerable number of
years.   His work was suggested by a slightly earlier work, the Life of
St Cuthbert by an anonymous monk of Lindisfarne, written not later than
705.   Canon Raine took as the authority for his text the 12th century
MS. in the Bodleian Library.   The MS. from which the suggestive reading
'Aluchfrith' for Alchfrith is taken, is in the British Museum, Cotton, Vesp.
D. vi.   It is an 11th century MS., but in Raine's opinion does not represent
so good and so early an original as the later Bodleian MS. does.   It gives
the Northumbrian pronunciation of Alchfrith's name, for an entry connects
it with Yorkshire.

The confusion between Cyniburg and Cuthburg may seem to be less
easily accounted for.   But when the men are confused the wives are
confused.   Besides, the story of Cyniburg and her sister Cyneswith and
their foundation of Castor is so very like the story of Cuthburg and her
sister Cuenburg and their foundation of Wimborne, that the confusion
between Cyniburg and Cuthburg became easy.   Further, it is interesting
to note that W. G. Searle in the Introduction to his important *Onomasticon
Anglo Saxonicum* (Cambridge 1897), p. xiv, in writing of "protothemes,"
says they were often confounded by the scribes.   He gives two examples,
Ælf and Æthel, in the first member of a personal name, and Cyne Cwen
and Coen.   I am inclined to think that here is an additional solution of
the difficulty created by William four hundred years after Eddi and Bede.
He certainly had not our means of keeping clear between these two ladies
or these two princes.

It is time to draw to a conclusion our consideration of the many
problems which the Bewcastle and Ruthwell Crosses provide and suggest.

If there has been throughout this essay a note of something like
confidence as to the early date assigned to the monuments, that has not

been due to any lack of appreciation of the difficulties which present themselves or have been discovered by opponents. Some of those difficulties are serious at first sight; others appear to me not serious at all; others remain serious, but their seriousness has been to some not inconsiderable extent modified. If it were not for the difficulties of archaeology, this present writer would long ago have left its study to others.

But, allowing to the full, and welcoming, the difficulties affecting the early date, it may fairly be said to have been established, in various writings on the subject, (1) that many of the objections raised have been completely refuted, (2) that some at least of them have been turned into serious arguments in favour of the early date, (3) that the rival date and origin suggested, David of Scotland at some such date as 1125, presents difficulties which its author would appear not to have appreciated at their full and fatal force. The remarkable unfittingness of that theory is equalled by the remarkable fittingness of the early date and origin. It may be added that the favourers of the early date feel prepared to meet—and would welcome—any fresh suggestion of a comparatively late date for the monuments which have so great a fascination for them, whatever the true date may be.

INDEX

Abercorn Cross, 25
Acca's Cross, 22, 36; his altar, 32
Acircius, Aldfrith, ch. VII
Adoration of the Magi, 59, 60
Adrian, 32
Aeft, aefter, 73–75
Aelflaed, 84
Agnellus, 58
Alchfrith, 5, 15, 28, 75, ch. VII
Alcuin, 24, 80, 81
Aldfrith, 71, ch. VII
Aldhelm, St, 21; churches, 20; crosses, 14;
    robe, 22
Alexander of Scotland, 52
Alexandria, 55, 57
Alfred's jewel, 72
Altars, 21, 34, 48
Alternative runes, 78–81
Aluchfrith, 76
Anglo-Saxon Chronicle, 72, 85
Anglo-Saxon MSS., irregularities, 73, 75, 77
Annunciation, the, 2, 11, 29, 60
Antecedent improbabilities, 49, 50
Antony, 31, 32
Archers, 32, 33
Archiepiscopos, 59
Arian crosses, 62
Arthurian legends, 8–11
Asgard, 33
Athelstan, 64
Auckland, 33
Aurona, church of, 61
Avalon, 8, 9

Bakewell, 33
Baldr, 33
Baldwin Brown, Professor, vi, 29, 30, 80
Baptism, the, 59
Bayeux Tapestry, 10, 23
Beard, the, 46
Bede, 32, 48, 68, 84, 87; his cross, 52
Bekn, 76
Bernicia, 47
Bethlehem, entry into, 60
Beverley, crosses at, 64
Bewcastle Cross, the, chequers, 36; Figure of
    Our Lord, 27; inscriptions, 4, 5, 16, 33,
    73–81; names, 15; patterns, 22, 36; pro-
    bable date, 5, 17; problems, 17; subjects,
    4, 36–40; sun-dial, 37; vine scrolls, 4, 36.
    See Runes
Birds, on coins, 30; on robes, 22; in sculpture,
    30, 31, 51
Biscop, 5, 6, 17, 18, 21, etc.
Blaecca, 20
Bologna, 63

Boniface of Crediton, 38–40
Book of Life, 85
Bosworth, A.-S. Dictionary, 75
Bradbourne, 33
Brandl, Professor, 69
Brescia, 62, 63
Bruton, marble altar, 21
Bugge, Sophus, 70
Burlington Magazine, vi
Burnsall, 50
Byzantium, 6, 55

Caedmon, 68, 70; at Ruthwell, 68–71; his
    cross, 52
Cana, feast at, 59, 60
Castor, 77, 88
Casts, 70
Cat Stane, the, 14
Cedd, 13, 69
Chad, 13
Charlemagne, 58
Chartres, 44, 45, 46, 61
Church-building, 18–21
Churchyards, 48, 49
Coins, 30, 79
Collingham, 74
Conway, Sir M., vi, 36
Cook, Mr A. B., 14
Cook, Professor A. S., vi, 3, 6, 26, 28, 29, 31,
    32, 33, 34, 37, 38, 39, 40, 42, 43, 44, 45,
    49, 50, 52, 54, 55, 61, 71, 73
Coptic art, 61
Crosses and altars, 48
Crosses, in pairs, 12; triple, 50; Abercorn,
    25; Acca's, 25, 36, 50; Aldhelm's, 14;
    Auckland, 33; Bakewell, 33; Beverley, 64;
    Bologna, 63, 64; Burnsall, 50; Collingham,
    74; Dewsbury, 51; Durham, 51; Ethel-
    wold's, 25, 50; Glastonbury, 8–11, 50; Irish,
    49; of James the Deacon, Hawkswell, 35;
    Lastingham, 51; Leeds, 31; Manx, 49;
    Monasterboice, 51; of Paulinus, 50; Sheffield,
    33; Whalley, 51; Wilfrith's, 49; Winwick, 51
Crucifixion, the, 2, 29
Culdees, the, 7, 31
Cunnyburrow, Lady, 77
Cuthbert, St, 25, 28, 45, 84, 88
Cuthburg, 85
Cwenburh, 85
Cyneswitha, 15
Cyniburga, 15, 75, 77

Dalton, Mr O. M., vi, 80
David of Scotland, 7, 51, 52
Dedication stone, Jarrow, 34
Deira, 5, 48

Dewsbury, 51
Dickins, Mr, vi
Didron, 44
Differences between Bewcastle and Ruthwell, 43, 47
Difficulties, 88, 89
Disney lectures, 1, 8, 33, 54, 59, 63, 71
Doge, the, 54–57
Domesday inquisitors, 69
Dragonesque sculpture, 10, 11, 25, 27, 41
Drahmal's Cross, 71, 72
Dream of the Rood, 4, 33, ch. VI
Durham, 51, 52

Ealdferth, 71
Ean, 76
Easingwold, 50
Eastern influence, 5, 21, 24, 28, 46, 61, 63
Ecgbert's Pontifical, 48
Ecgfrith, 14, 18, 41, ch. VII
Eddi, Stephen, 18, 75, 83, 84, 87, 88
Edwin, 19
Eldfridus, 71
Entry into Jerusalem, 60
Etheldreda, 35
Ethelwold, 25, 50

Falconry, 38, 39
Fegan, fogan, 69
Felix Ravenna, 56
Flight into Egypt, the, 29
Florence of Worcester, 86
Forbes, Mr, vi
Foreign artists and workmen, 6, 17, 19, 22, 23, 24, 47, 48
Freising, von, 80
Fridegoda, 85

Galla Placidia, 18, 63
Gaul, 6
Gessus Kristtus, 76
Gibson, Mr, vii
Glastonbury, obelisks and crosses at, 8–11
Gollancz, Dr, 67
Gospel-book, 19, 19 *n.*, 25, 26
Greek Popes, 47
Gregory, Pope, 31
Guess-work, 24, 25
Guide stones, 12
Guinevere, 9, 10

Haddenham, 35
Hadrian, 32
Hawking, 38
Hawkswell, 35
Healing of the Blind, 2, 60
Hefenfeld, 47
Henry I of England, 7, 43
Henry II of England, 7, 10
Hewison, Dr, vi, ch. VII
Hexham, 18
Holy Rood, Dream of the, 4, 33, ch. VI
Horsa, 14
Howorth, Sir H., vii

Ini, 9, 85
Inscriptions, 2, 3, 4, 30, 33, 73–78

Insulated ideas, 23
Interlacements, 4, 25, 27, 28, 52
Ivory chair, ch. V

Jarrow, 6, 34
Jedburgh, sculpture at, 7, 8
Jupiter columns, 14

Keary, Mr, 30
Kedmon, 71
Kentwine, king, 8
Kin, Kyn. *See* Cyn
Kirkdale, 37

Lamb, the, symbolism of, 62, 63
Later runes, 78–81
Leeds Cross, the, 31
Lethaby, Professor, vi, 30, 35
Liber Vitae, 85
Lincoln, 8
Lindisfarne, 5, 8, 17, 45
Local pronunciation, 69
Logeman, Dr, 71
Loki, 33
Lombards, history and art, 23, 58
Lul, 81
Lyon, 5, 6

Maclagan, Mr Eric, 46, 70
Magi, 59
Mahommed, 23, 47
Malmesbury, 14, 20; William of, 8, 14
Manger, the, 60
Manx runes, 74
Marriage at Cana, 59, 60
Martyrology, 32
Maximianus, 28, 29, ch. V
Maximus, 56
Margaret of Scotland, 7, 51, 52
Milan, 61
Mistakes, 25, 77, 78
Monograms, 57–59
Multiplication of the Loaves, 59, 60

Naiton, 41
New Testament subjects, 62
Nimbus, the, 43–45
Nonantola, 34
North-side, superstition, 21

O, lozenge-shaped, 34
Onomasticon Anglo Saxonicum, 88
Osgyð, 79, 80
Oswald, St, 5, 47, 68
Oswin, Onswin, 74
Oswy, Osuio, 6, 15, 74
Othona, 69
Otto III, ch. V
Our Lord's Figure on the Crosses, 26
Ovin, 35

Palaeography, 33
Paul and Antony, 31, 32
Paulinus, 20, 50, 51
Peada, Pada, 30, 79
Peers, Mr C. H., 7
Phonetic spelling, 69

Pictish patterns, 25, 41, 52
Pictures, Biscop's, 21
Portable altars, 33, 34, 48
Problems, puzzling, 17
Pronunciation, local, 69
Pyramids at Glastonbury, 8–11

Quinisext Council, 63, 68

Raine, Canon, 88
Ravenna, 22, 28, 29, ch. v
Reality of Our Lord's sufferings, 63
Regin, 31
Reims, 44
Ripon, 18, 19
Rivoira, Commendatore, 6, 17, 22, 24, 26, 28, 36, 52, 62
Robes of Our Lord, 45
Rome, vine scrolls in, 60; visited by Wilfrith and Biscop, 5, 6
Rubbings, advantage of, 16, 69
Runes, 3, 4, 8, 16, 17, 30, 31, 38, 40, 69, 78–82; table of, 82
Ruthwell Cross, Figure of Our Lord, 27; inscriptions, 2–4, 33, 66, 67, 69–73, 77; probable date, 5, 42; subjects, 2, 28–36; tradition and history, 42; two shafts, 45

Sagas, 31
Salona, 56, 57
Salzburg MS., 80
Samaritan Woman, the, 60
Sandbach Crosses, 11–13
Sca Maria, at York, 46
Sceattas, 30
School of Art in Northumbria, 27
Searle, Rev. W. G., 88
Sheffield, 33
Sherborne, 14, 20
Sigurd, 31
Solomon's throne, 55
Somerset, sculptures in, 10
Spalato, 8, 56, 57
Squeezes, 69
S. Salvatore, 62
St Aldhelm, 14, 20, 21, 22
St Andrews, 52
St Cuthbert, 25, 28, 45
Stencil plates, 41
Stephens, Professor George, 16, 70
St John Baptist, 28, 44, 60
Stokes, Miss, 44

Stone churches, 19, 20
St Oswald, 5, 47
St Paul's London, 8
St Vigeans, 41
Sun-dial, 37
S. Vitale, 54, 63

Table of Anglian runes, 82
Tassell, Mr, vii
Tatbert, 87
Tavolette, subjects of, 59, 60
Theodore, archbishop, 32; of Milan, 61
Theodota, tombstone of, 23
Thornhill, 74, 76
Thun, thynne, 73
Tica, abbat, 8, 10
Trial by Water, 59
Triple crosses, 50
Trumberecht, disputed tombstone, 24
Turgot, 51, 52
Type and anti-type, 21, 28

Ungget, 77
Upton, 76

Venice, 54, 57, 65
Vercelli, 72
Vetta and Victis, 14
Vietor, 17, 70, 71
Vigfusson, 70
Vine scrolls, 4, 22, 27, 29, 33, 55, 60
Visitation, the, 29, 50
Vitale, S., 54, 63
Vitalian, 19 *n.*
Void spaces, 3

Walker, Mr Emery, vii
Washing the Feet, 2, 28
Wearmouth, 6
Whalley, 51
Whitby, conference at, 5, 82
Wilfrith, 5, 17, 18, 19, 22, 46, 47, 87, etc.
William of Malmesbury, 8, 14, 50, 86
Wimborne, 85, 88
Wirksworth, 63
Worcester, Florence of, 86
Wulfhere, 16

Yarm, tombstone at, 24
York Powell, 70
York, School of, 80, 81
Ythancester, 69

Plate I

IVORY CHAIR OF MAXIMIANUS AT RAVENNA

I

Plate II

IVORY CHAIR OF MAXIMIANUS AT RAVENNA

2

Emery Walker Ph sc.

Plate III

IVORY CHAIR OF MAXIMIANUS AT RAVENNA

3

Plate IV

5. Jedburgh

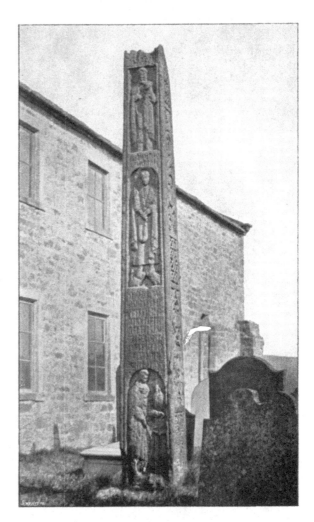

4. Bewcastle

6. The Bewcastle Shaft

Plate V

8. The Ruthwell Cross

9. The Ruthwell Cross

7. The Bewcastle Shaft

Plate VI

10. Grave-cover, Wirksworth

13. Acca's Cross, Hexham

11. Vine Scroll

12. Trumberht

Plate VII

15. The Sandbach Crosses

17. The Kirkdale Dial

14. Dedication Stone, Jarrow

16. Cross-head, Durham